PRAISE FOR TH
MEANS BUSINESS

C000004284

'Practical, insightful and incredibly useful. Alison Jones is the trusted friend everyone should have when writing a business book. Combining her unique connections and expertise in the worlds of writing, publishing and business-building, she writes with clarity, generosity and wit, distilling the best of her experience - and that of a whole host of successful business authors - into an incredibly useful guide for anyone looking to write a book that really works for their business.' – *Grace Marshall, Head coach, chief encourager and productivity ninja, author of* How To Be Really Productive

'Here's another lesson: blurbs don't actually sell books. But if they did, this one would help you decide that this is a worthy primer, a great place to start on your journey to make a business book that matters.' – *Seth Godin, author and blogger*

'In this comprehensive, well-researched and immensely helpful book, Alison Jones lays out everything you need to know about how to write the right book, in the right way, to drive business results. Whether you've toyed with the idea of writing a book for years, and never gotten off the starting line, or you've already written several books, but want to do it in a more pleasant, purposeful and high-impact way next time, this book is for you.' – *Amanda Setili, president, Setili & Associates business consulting, and author of* Fearless Growth

I

'What Alison Jones doesn't know about writing, publishing and marketing business books probably isn't worth knowing. Even if the cover price of this book were £100, you'd still be getting a bargain: the sheer volume of advice it contains will prove priceless to anyone thinking of writing a business book. It contains everything you need to know, and then some.' – *Scott Pack, author of* How to Perfect Your Submission: Tips from a publisher

'Alison's book club is indeed extraordinary – in style, practical how-tos and sheer entertainment. I love it.' – *David Taylor, author of* The Naked Leader

'At last! The Writers' & Artists' Yearbook has a companion. Read them both. Do what they say. And be lucky.' – *Dr Andy Cope, author of* Now That's What I Call Leadership *and* The Art of Being Brilliant

'Writing a book helps you share your ideas with the world - and become recognized for them in the marketplace. Alison Jones's informative new guide enables you to craft a meaningful work that will have a lasting impact on your business success.' – *Dorie Clark, author of* Entrepreneurial You *and* Stand Out, *and adjunct professor, Duke University Fuqua School of Business*

'Unlike many people in business, I generally have an aversion to business books other than Dilbert. What I can't bear - and don't believe - is the idea that any one author has all the answers, or at least enough to hold my attention for 200 plus pages. *This Book Means Business* is a much better recipe for success, and has extracted top tips from over 100 people with a veritable salmagundi of experience and talent. Alison Jones is a master compiler and curator of case studies and, as a result, this book about business has fantastic practical and pragmatic value for anyone in the business of books, and beyond.' – *David Roche, author, former President of the Booksellers Association, Chair of New Writing North and non-executive director of The London Book Fair*

'Writing a book is a big deal, but it's not rocket science. In her podcast and in this book Alison has demystified the process by revealing exactly how dozens of successful authors have gone about it. This book is full of ideas that work: open it at any page and you'll find something you can use.' – *Patrick Vlaskovits, New York Times bestselling author of* Hustle *and* The Lean Entrepreneur

'Alison Jones brings her in-depth knowledge of business strategy to the topic of writing a business book, delving deep into the psychology of writing as well as providing tips and tactics on the practical side. A fantastic guide for those who want to take their business – and writing – to the next level.' – *Joanna Penn, bestselling author, podcaster, and award-winning creative entrepreneur, www.TheCreativePenn.com*

'Bad news: there are a lot of books on self-publishing. Great news: Alison's book is brilliant because it's not just about publishing your book - it's about growing yourself, your platform, your network, and your business around your book. Buy *This Book Means Business* right now and follow Alison's wise and detailed advice at every step. The book - and the business - you build will thank you for it!' – *David Newman, author of* Do It! Marketing

'Alison Jones has done a remarkable thing – she has created a toolkit that will transform your life and your business. *This Book Means Business takes a practical approach to planning, writing and marketing your book which applies her experience as a publisher and writer, and draws on the best mentors* from the business of writing business books. Follow her advice and prepare for your life to change as you accelerate your personal and professional development.' – *Bec Evans, innovation consultant and co-founder of Prolifiko*

'Every now and then a new book gets released, and you find yourself facepalming while saying aloud, "Now, why couldn't the author have written this 5 years ago?!" This is exactly the reaction I had to Alison's *This Book Means Business*. It's so jam-packed full of such vital information, any number of tips would have influenced my writing and publishing journey. Not only that, but Alison has built upon this with some incredible business insights from business giants across the globe. I can't change the past, but this book will change my future writing career, that's for sure.' – *Robin Waite, author of* Online Business Startup *and* Take Your Shot

'This book is the total package! It's really not easy to find a book that covers both the "why" and the "how" of writing a business book – usually it's one or the other, and very often only the "how" in fact. Alison Jones's book covers both. The guidance she gives each step of the way is so detailed, it's amazing the amount of things you would overlook if you didn't have this book handy to support you on your writing journey. Indispensable!' – *Melissa Romo, Director of Global Content at Sage, author and publisher*

'If you want to write a business book, *This Book Means Business* gives you a blueprint to get ideas out of your head and into the bookstore.' – *Pam Didner, speaker and marketing consultant, author of* Global Content Marketing

THIS BOOK MEANS BUSINESS

Clever ways to plan and write a book that works harder for your business

ALISON JONES

First published in Great Britain by Practical Inspiration Publishing, 2018

ISBN 9781910056691 (print)
ISBN 9781910056684 (ebook – Kindle)
ISBN 9781910056752 (ebook – ePub)

Practical Inspiration
PUBLISHING

For Dad, who taught me how to make the perfect cup of tea.

TABLE OF CONTENTS

FOREWORD

If I had a dollar for every person who asked me whether writing a book will make them rich, I'd be able to confirm that it did. The reality is there are better reasons for writing your book than expecting to get rich through selling it. Yes, some authors get six-figure advances, sell millions of copies and get on bestseller lists. But they are firmly in the minority. You need to find your reason to write. Whether it's the people you want to help, the art you want to create or the legacy you want to leave, that reason will keep your bum on the seat and fingers on the keys.

Writing for an audience makes you notice things. It clarifies your thinking and helps you to come up with solutions the world has been waiting for. Writing your book will prepare you to speak on your topic with authority and help you to question, then improve your ideas. You'll create habits that serve you in other aspects of your life and astonish yourself in the process.

Many of the benefits you'll get on the journey from blank page to Amazon and beyond will be like the best surprise—which by its very nature you can't engineer.

The dream of writing a book is hardly ever about the 'writing' part. It's almost always about the 'holding your book in your hands' part. And while it's lovely to see your name on the spine of a book on the shelf alongside those of authors you admire, what's even better is the feeling you'll get when someone emails you out of the blue one day to tell you that your book changed their life. Trust me—they will. You almost certainly have nagging doubts as you ride the seesaw between permission and hubris. Maybe you're worried that your idea isn't unique or that it's all been said before. But one thing is for sure: it may have been said before, but it hasn't been said by you.

And if you're worrying that you're 'not a writer', don't. Nobody would be more surprised to know I'm an author than my high school English teacher, Miss McGinley. She tried and failed for five years to get me to 'fulfil my potential' and coax me out of my mostly 'solid C grade' mindset. It wasn't until three years later when I had a reason to go back and work for that 'A' that I discovered I could write.

'They' – the people responsible for imparting worldly wisdom – say the only workout you regret is the one you didn't do. The same holds true for writing a book. In the words of my friend Seth Godin; 'You don't need more time, you just need to decide.' And now that you have, Alison is on hand with decades of knowledge, experience and wisdom, not mention the secrets of all the successful business book authors she's grilled in The Extraordinary Business Book Club, to show you how it's done.

You don't have a moment to waste.

Bernadette Jiwa, author of *Story Driven*, *Hunch*,
Difference, *Marketing: A Love Story* and more
www.thestoryoftelling.com
February 2018

PREFACE

You'll find in these pages a selection of tools, techniques and tips on the business of writing business books. Some I've developed myself for my own use or that of my clients, or adapted from a long career in publishing innovation and senior management; most are drawn from interviews with world-class writers in the Extraordinary Business Book Club podcast: www.extraordinarybusinessbooks.com

All have been tested by real business people writing real books. And they all work, although they won't all work for every person in every situation.

I can promise you that wherever you're at in your book-writing journey – whatever problem you've come up against, however stuck you feel you are – there will be something here to help.

But it's not just about getting you unstuck.

This book is designed to help you make writing your book a profitable business activity, so that you see a return on your investment of time and energy long before publication. This period of writing is itself a fantastic opportunity to build your visibility and your network.

I guarantee you'll find an idea you can start using today to make your book work for your business, whatever stage it's at. I've tried all these tips and techniques myself and each one has moved me along in my thinking, writing or business development.

I'd love to hear what works for you, and how you've adapted these ideas to suit your own book and business. You can share in the Extraordinary Business Book Club group on Facebook, send me a tweet @bookstothesky, or drop me an email at hello@alisonjones.com.

And if you've developed your own brilliant way of building your business as you write your book, maybe you can be the next guest on the podcast!

Alison Jones
February 2018

INTRODUCTION

'The book that will change your life the most is the book you write.' – Seth Godin

Why are you thinking of writing a book? To become the go-to expert in your field, to get speaking gigs, to create a passive revenue stream?

All excellent reasons. But if you're focused on what the book will do for you once it's published, you're missing a trick.

This Book Means Business shows you how to get the most out of the process of planning, researching and writing your book, so that it works for you and your business right from the start.

Because if you're going to spend all those hours writing a book, you might as well maximize your return on investment in as many areas as possible, as early as possible.

This book is all about treating the writing of YOUR book as part of your business, making it happen one little bit of profile-raising, network-building, revenue-generating, search-engine-optimizing content at a time.

I've not just written this book, I've lived it. Most of the material has been developed through my podcast – the Extraordinary Business Book Club – in which I invite writers, publishers, and others with something interesting to say about the business of business books to share their experience.

Over the months I've spent planning and writing it, it has become the engine of my personal and professional growth. Personally it's driven self-development, productivity and strategic thinking, not to mention the benefit to my own writing practice; professionally that has translated into network development, a stronger offline and online platform, and ultimately a better business. All before it was even finished, let alone published.

And that's what I want for you too.

The business book growth spiral

There's a beautiful natural expression of this self-reinforcing, exponential model: the growth spiral. It's also known as the equiangular spiral, the logarithmic spiral, or, as Swiss mathematician Jacob Bernoulli put it, *Spira mirabilis*, 'the marvellous spiral'.

The growth spiral is both a mathematical and an organic concept. It's found in nature at every scale: the nerves in your cornea, the buds of a Romanesco broccoli head, the curve of a nautilus shell, the flung-out arms of a galaxy.

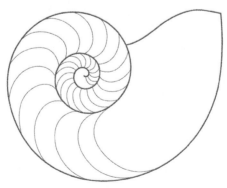

Nautilus shell

It's logical yet instinctive, and it's the perfect expression of the business book-writing journey, embracing all aspects of personal and professional growth.

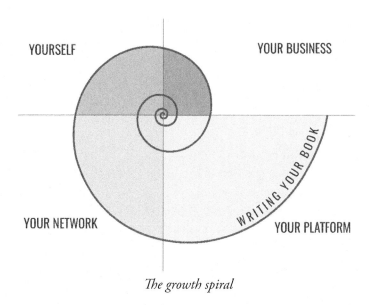

The growth spiral

Part 1 of this book explores the four segments of that quadrant in turn, showing how your book can help you develop each one.

Growing your business

Your business is the economic expression of your passion and personality in the world, and it is also the 'back-end' of your book, as Michael E. Gerber puts it.

For most writers – novelists and most non-fiction authors – the book is the end product. For business-book writers there's a different dynamic: the business underpins the book, and the book is successful only if it succeeds in building the business. (This puts us in a much better position financially than those other writers, as one big new client that signs up because of the book will almost certainly bring in more revenue overnight than most book sales will in a year.)

In this section you'll discover how to make sure the two are aligned so that your book becomes an integral part of the business, your best salesperson, working while you sleep and always on message.

Growing your platform

('Platform' is a hideous word, almost as bad as 'content', but until someone comes up with a better alternative we're stuck with it. Sorry.)

At Speakers' Corner in Hyde Park, London, anyone can come along and speak about any topic. If they want to be seen and heard, though, they bring a stepladder or box to stand on, to raise them above the heads of those around them so they can be seen and heard by more people.[1]

Your platform, like that ladder, is what raises you above the noise of the crowd. It allows you to grab and hold people's attention, and get them to listen to what you have to say. Each business book author's platform is different, but, with so many tools available to help you get your message out, there's no excuse for seeing your book as your only route to the reader.

---

[1] In 2017 soapboxes and ladders were banned from Speakers' Corner for health and safety reasons. Better build your platform some other way.

Unlike Speakers' Corner – where you have no control over who happens to be passing – you can set up your online and offline platform to get your message in front of the people you're interested in talking to. But the basic principle of Speakers' Corner still holds true: if you want people to stop and listen you'd better have something interesting to say, and you'd better say it well. In the 'platform' section you'll find ideas for using your book as the engine of your content marketing strategy, increasing visibility and engagement, and even leveraging other people's platforms to punch above your weight.

Growing your network

Your professional relationships are at the heart of your business, and they come in a variety of flavours. There are your core relationships: existing clients, your closest social media communities and your email list, which will also include – hopefully – some raving fans. Then there are partners and suppliers, peers, network coordinators and connectors, mentors, and other contacts such as friendly journalists or people in related industries.

There's also a whole group of people you don't have a relationship with right now, but you'd like to – e.g. future clients, the rockstars in your field – most of whom will be connected either directly or indirectly to someone in your existing network. Facebook recently disproved the old story that we're separated from anyone else on the planet by only six degrees of separation – apparently it's now just over three and a half degrees on average.[2]

---

[2] https://research.fb.com/three-and-a-half-degrees-of-separation/

When you're writing a book, your position in this web of relationships shifts. Suddenly you're leading the conversation, and that changes the way others relate to you. In the 'network' section of this book you'll find ideas for using this change of state creatively to develop and deepen relationships strategically.

Growing yourself

There's a good reason why so many self-development gurus recommend journaling: the act of writing reflectively is a powerful tool to help synthesize experience, clarify your thinking and develop your ideas.

Psychologist Roberta Satow puts it this way:

'Writing promotes the development of my self because seeing what I have written and responding to it makes me aware of what I am thinking and feeling and engages me in my own internal process.' [3]

In the section on growing yourself, you'll discover how you can use the writing of your book to improve your habits and productivity, the clarity of your thinking, and how you conceive, structure and present your ideas (for the book and beyond).

But how do you actually write the book that will catalyze growth in all these areas? Most entrepreneurs are not professional writers – why should they be? – so Part 2, 'Writing your book', brings together the collective wisdom

---

[3] www.psychologytoday.com/blog/life-after-50/201707/writing-self-development

and experience of those who've done it before – to help with the nitty-gritty of getting the damn thing written, from planning through overcoming procrastination to polishing the first draft.

Is it time for you to write a book?

Your book doesn't begin with the Introduction; it starts with your vision for your life and your business. Getting clear on that isn't a one-off job, because what you want from life evolves, and your understanding of your own message will shift and deepen over time.

Supercoach Michael Neill warned me against writing a book too soon, or in his words, 'premature articulation':

> 'We try and put words to it before we've really felt it...
> There is a time to write. I know for me, the timing of
> my books is tied in to some movement in me.'

Don't leave it too late, either. It's possible to end up writing what you used to believe, or something that you know is true but doesn't excite you any more.

My dad taught me how to make the perfect cup of tea: use fresh water and wait until the water's come to a rolling boil. Don't pour it too soon, before it's boiling, and don't wait until it's switched itself off and started to cool (or even worse when the water's been reheated a few times and is stale). If you can catch that moment when you've deeply felt and experienced what you're writing about but before you've lost your excitement about it, you're onto a winner.

Graham Allcott, author of *How to be a Productivity Ninja*, put it this way:

> 'Go out and do the work first and then put the work into a book later. I think it's important to have a backstory and a credibility to bring to the book… If I can say, "I've taught Outlook to Bill Gates and timekeeping to the Swiss and efficiency to the Germans," well, there's a great start. It gives you more credibility when you're in the room with people and when someone picks the book off the shelf. More importantly, it makes the book better because it gives you the experience of all of those conversations.'

Caroline Webb, author of *How to Have a Good Day*, echoes this, pointing out the value of the interplay between the book she was writing, and the work she was doing day by day as she wrote:

> 'That iteration between the writing and the clients, that's been central to the way this whole project came together over the years. The client work has made the writing so much more practical [and] the writing has really sharpened my ideas as I'm working with clients.'

If it's time, if you've done the work and built the backstory, if your ideas have been tested in the real world and you're ready to articulate them to people who've not even met you yet (but really need to), but you're struggling with the fear, lack of clarity or lack of time, then this book is for you. Dip in and out, experiment, have fun, and let me know what works for you and what you discover at hello@alisonjones.com.

A NOTE ON FEAR

If you're reading this book, you probably haven't actually written your book yet.

And, if you're anything like me, it's because when you sit down to write the book of your business – the book that articulates the message you most care about to the people you most want to reach – the blankness of the page, the significance of the task and the fear of messing it up stops you dead. I spent nearly two years failing to write this book – and I've written five others before in a fraction of that time for other people and purposes.

The fear around writing a book is so vast and multifaceted that it merits a whole book in its own right: fear of failure, fear of success, fear of visibility, fear of not being good enough or original enough, fear of criticism or ridicule, fear of committing to one idea. Often the fear operates incognito: it disguises itself as procrastination or perfectionism and, while we beat ourselves up for not getting the job done, fear congratulates itself on keeping us safe by keeping us small.

As with anything in life, it all starts with a decision: the decision to dare.

Most people simply don't dare start a business – you've already done that.

Most people don't dare write a book – but you're not most people.

I can't take away the fear, and I'm not sure I'd want to (it serves a useful purpose), but what I have tried to do in this book is give you tools to manage it. It's reassuring to discover that every author is fearful, and helpful to discover how they went ahead and wrote the book anyway. And when you take the approach I set out here it inoculates you against fear one tiny bite at a time – one blog post, one talk, one conversation – rather than saving it all up for launch time.

'Fear is excitement without breath,' said business journalist Robert Heller. So breathe, as deeply and as often as necessary, and keep reading.

A NOTE ON PUBLISHING OPTIONS

There's never been a more exciting time to be an author or an entrepreneur, and if you're an author who's also an entrepreneur you just hit the jackpot. Ten years ago you'd have had little choice but to submit your book proposal to an agent or traditional publisher – or more likely 30 of them – and hope one of them liked it enough to make you an offer. And if they did, they'd have the last say on the format, cover design, price, publication date and so on, and you'd get a modest cut of royalty revenue.

Today, however, you have options. And if you've established your platform, built a following and control your own routes to market, those options are very interesting indeed.

Many authors who could secure a traditional publishing deal with ease are choosing to exercise those options. Here's how it worked for Graham Allcott, author of *How to be a Productivity Ninja*:

> 'I turned down the deal with [the publisher] because they wanted far too much control over the whole process. Literally, the day before I got on the plane to Sri Lanka, I said, "I'm going to go off and write this book, and I'll talk to you when I get back about whether this is something I do through you." Then, I sat

there writing the book, and I had this one particular thing I wanted to say. It was [a] little bit on the edge and risky and I remember thinking, "What will the publisher think about me writing this? Will they take that out?" It was at that moment, I thought, "Screw the publisher. I'm going to write the book for me. I'm going to write the book that I want to write."'

He published the book himself. It was a huge success, and it was then taken up by Icon Books and published traditionally, but with Graham's input and on his terms.

At its simplest, publishing today is a three-way choice:

traditional model – publisher pays all the costs of publication and owns exclusive rights to publish, has final decision on publishing decisions, author receives a royalty on sales and can buy copies for own use at discount. Result: professional quality book focused on maximizing returns to publisher.

self-publishing – author pays publication costs, retains all rights and makes all decisions, can purchase author copies at cost and keeps all revenue from sales. Result: quality of book depends on expertise of author and/or professionals used, control is with author.

partnership publishing – author works with professional publisher to produce book, pays publication costs. Rights, degree of control, cost of author copies and revenue splits from sales vary widely, so check the small print carefully. At its best, this can give authors the best of all worlds.

I've worked in traditional publishing for most of my career, but I set up Practical Inspiration Publishing as a partnership: my authors' books need to serve their business rather than mine, and it's my job to make sure they do that successfully. I'm proud to say that several of my authors rejected traditional publishing deals to work with me because they preferred my more collaborative approach.

However you're planning to publish your book, or even if you're not sure yet, this book is designed to help you write a book that's as successful for your business as it is for your readers.

Part 1

YOUR BUSINESS AND YOU

GROWING YOUR BUSINESS

'I've had development managers whose job is to get out there and talk to people, you know, open relationships and generate business. Realistically, if a business development manager was incredibly driven, they could possibly be out there doing that job 1,600 hours per year and a lot of that would be wasted time. As a business you'd spend something like £50,000 putting someone into that role. They may not get the message right. They may need a training period. They may have sick days. They may become awesome and leave and go work somewhere else... I look at this idea of 1,600 hours that they could spend, and I simply think, "Well, what if I just print 1,600 books and send them out to all the same people at a fraction of the cost?" And it actually kind of does the same job.'
– Daniel Priestley

Or as sales and marketing guru Marcus Sheridan puts it: 'Great content is the best sales tool in the world.'

But if your book is going to work effectively for your business it needs to be deeply integrated and aligned with it, and that's what this section is all about. We're going to start with some big questions that take you right upstream because, if you're not clear on where your business is going, you're not ready to write the book to move it forwards.

what's your why? or the 20-year perspective

One of my favourite tools for business thinking isn't one of the fancy models I learned on my MBA; it's a poem by Rudyard Kipling:

> *I keep six honest serving-men*
> *(They taught me all I knew);*
> *Their names are What and Why and When*
> *And How and Where and Who.*

And it all starts with WHY.

What's the 20-year vision for your business? That's probably further ahead than you're used to thinking. Clients often laugh nervously when I ask them this question. But if you're thinking of writing a book it's a sensible question to ask yourself: after all, books can have a very long shelf life.

Why does it matter? Well, if you want to sell the business eventually, you'll do things differently to someone who wants a lifestyle business that ends with them. If you want to establish a methodology and train other trainers to deliver your system, you've got to start establishing your intellectual property base and systematizing things. If you want to be working with very different clients to those you're working with now, or in a different area, you need to be thinking about where and how that shift starts before you put pen to paper.

There's something freeing about 20 years, too. If I were to ask you about your 12-month goals you'd give me SMART targets that take what you're currently doing one step further. They'd be hedged around with constraints and hobbled by realism. In 20 years though? That's different. You could do anything in 20 years, right?

And that's the point: if you could do anything, *what would it be?*

Once you've articulated that 20-year vision, you can pull your time horizon in a little, keeping that end in mind, and focus on where you want your business to be in say five years' time. Now you can be specific: think about how you'll be spending your day, where you'll be located, how many staff you'll have, what products and services you'll be offering, who your clients will be, what turnover and profit you'll be making.

Once you know where you're going, you need to work out the route to take you there, because without the route you don't have a strategy, only a vision.

'Our goals can only be reached through the vehicle of a plan, in which we must fervently believe, and upon which we must vigorously act. There is no other route to success.' – Pablo Picasso

A vision is a great start, the best start, but you also need to know how you'll achieve that: what specific strengths and opportunities will drive you forward? How will you overcome your weaknesses and manage your threats? How will you differentiate yourself from your competitors? Which clients will you target and how will you reach them? What mix of products and services will be in your portfolio?

So now let's get really real: what are your goals for this year? If you've already set goals, take a look at them in the light of the thinking you've just done – do they still stand or do they need some adjustment? If you haven't yet set goals then this is the ideal time: you should have much more clarity now on where you're going and what you want to achieve.

And finally, think about which strands of your business you need to focus on to get you there. You may need to drop some products or services that are no longer serving you, to give you time and headspace to build up the others.

Your book needs a clear strategic purpose within this bigger picture. It must align with the WHY of your business if it's going to be an effective tool to help you achieve it.

Most fundamentally, you need to be writing to reach the right readers (see **target reader**). But that's not all. Is the book a one-off or a series reflecting a whole stream of business activity? If you're building up your training programme, how can you link the book to that, for example as preparatory reading? Is the main purpose to get speaking engagements, in which case what is your best 'hook'?

Over to you

- What's your 20-year vision for your business, and what does that mean for your book?
- What specific products and services will your book support, and how?

---

target reader – who are you writing for?

One of the insights that typically falls out of the **20-year vision** work is a clearer understanding of who it is you want to work with in the future. They may or they may not be the same as the people you're currently working with. If you want to reach people you don't have access to right now, why not use your book to help you make that step?

There's an obvious synergy: a key part of business strategy is focusing on your customer, and a key part of writing a book is focusing on your reader.

And ideally, your ideal client *is the same as* your ideal reader. Just think about that for a moment. Your book is an opportunity to talk directly and at length to the very person you most want to come and work with you. If you can convince them that this is the book for them, if they feel once they've read it that you understand them, if they like and trust you, the book will have achieved more than a million-dollar advertising budget could ever do.

Many business owners resist the idea of focusing on a particular market segment because they think they're reducing their potential client base, and it's exactly the same with books – I can't tell you the number of proposals I saw as a commissioning editor that identified the target market as 'the general reader'. Sorry, but there's no such thing.

It might be true that anyone who reads your book will get something out of it but for most books by most authors – and certainly those without a big PR machine behind them – the more focused the book's market the easier it will be for you to write, the more useful it will be for your readers, and the more likely it will be that those readers will find the book in the first place and make the decision to buy it.

You might find yourself in the position of writing for someone other than your target client: one of my authors is writing her book for women in middle management but her ideal client is a HR manager. She's using the book to pitch to HR managers to run workshops for their staff and, by building a community of individual managers who've read and loved the draft, she's getting introductions and referrals to the corporate gatekeepers who decide how to spend the training budget.

So if you think you've got that kind of complexity or mismatch between your ideal client and your ideal reader don't panic – just spend some time planning how the two will work together.

Over to you

- Who do you want to work with in the future?
- What market sector is your book aimed at?
- If these two are different, why is that and what can you do about it?

target reader – the persona

It's not enough just to be clear on your target market: books are read by people, not market segments. So think of your target reader as an individual.

When they're designing a new system, software developers create a persona for each of their target user types. Then whenever they have to make a decision about design or functionality they check first: what would Jon/Lisa/Howard/Mavis make of this? You can use exactly the same principle to help you write a more compelling, readable book.

There's something powerful about focusing on one person. Have you ever watched a report from a disaster scene? The reporter talks about the terrible loss of life and devastation and you think, 'How awful.' But it's not until the camera turns onto a child, standing desolate in the ruins of his home with no idea where his parents are, that it really affects you. We're wired to connect to individuals, not concepts. So creating an emotional connection with an individual, even a fictional individual, is a powerful way of keeping you engaged and engaging as you write.

I'm writing this book for Dee, although she doesn't know it. There's a picture of her stuck to the wall above my desk. She stops me writing for myself, and she keeps reminding me to stick to the point – that's nice, she says, but what's in it for me? You can create more than one persona if you have more than one core target market but don't go crazy – the more you have, the less you can focus on any one.

Here's how to construct a basic persona for your target reader:

9

1. If you could only have one reader for your book, who would it be and why? Get as clear as possible about what the book will do for that person, and what that person will do for you.
2. Define some of the characteristics of that person: location, age, job type/level, gender, family situation, hobbies, even what car they drive and where they go on holiday!
3. Think about what motivates that person: what are their key fears?
4. What are their daily frustrations?
5. What are their desires: what is it they want to achieve?
6. How can you help them most effectively? (Use their words, not yours.)
7. Where are they currently trying to source the information or services they need, online and offline?
8. How can you reach them, online and offline? What communities, groups, networks do they engage in?
9. What more do you need to know about them? How can you find out?

It may sound whimsical to ask where your target reader goes on holiday but it works: the clearer you are about the person you're trying to reach, the more clearly you'll be able to speak to them in a way that floats their boat. (It's also incredibly useful when it comes to putting together a marketing plan, but that's a whole different book.)

It's so easy to forget when you're an expert in something, when you've spent years learning the language and using the tools and techniques, that the people you're writing for don't even know what they don't know. They won't use the same words as you do, they won't care about the finer points of your art like you do: all they know is that something's wrong and they're looking for someone who can help.

Another useful tool to help you better understand and serve your reader is the empathy map, created by Dave Gray, which helps you go deeper into the day-to-day experience of your reader, inviting you to explore what they think and feel, see, hear, and say and do, and what their key pain points and desired gains are.

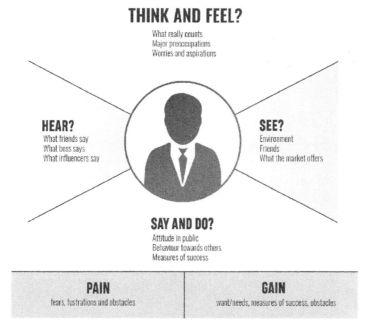

Empathy map (originally created by Dave Gray of XPLANE)

Over to you

- Give your ideal reader a name – real or made-up – and complete the list of questions above for him or her. What do you learn about how to write your book from the answers? Find a suitable picture to represent them and stick it on your wall to remind you exactly who it is you're writing for.
- Create an empathy map for that reader – what does that reveal about how you need to write, structure or pitch your book?

write the right book – Venn diagram

Even if you're crystal clear on who it is you're writing for and why, there's any number of books you COULD write for them. How do you choose between them? You can find yourself in perpetual possibility procrastination – unable to settle down to write one book because, as soon as you do, another brilliant potential title springs to mind.

It's tempting to stick your fingers in your ears and try to focus on the book you've started writing, but it's better in the long run to give yourself the space and time you need to explore your ideas.

So go ahead and generate as many possible titles as you can, as long as (and this is important) they all fulfil two criteria:

1. they fit with your business strategy as revealed in your 20-year vision, and
2. they are designed to appeal to the ideal reader you identified in your persona.

Here's a simple model to help you come up with ideas for books in your 'sweet spot': at the intersection of your expertise, your customers' needs, and your broader business strategy.

On a piece of paper draw three circles in the form of a Venn diagram:

'Sweet spot' Venn diagram

Alongside the circle entitled 'my expertise', write down a list of the professional skills/areas that you could possibly write about. You might need to do more research for some, that's fine. But the starting point is what you bring to the party. (Most authors start and end here: having identified a book topic on which they can speak with authority, they start writing. That's not strategic thinking.)

Secondly, alongside the 'customers' needs' circle, write a list of the questions you are most frequently asked, the concerns and problems that bring customers to you, the needs – well articulated or barely understood – that they look to you to meet.

Finally, look ahead. The future circle has three inter-related parts:

1. Your industry – what trends and technologies are emerging? How will these change your sector in the short to medium term? How is the old order changing, and what new opportunities are arising?
2. Your business – in the light of these changes, where are you taking your business over the next five years? What are the areas of focus and growth, and are you planning to extend or develop into new areas?
3. Your customers – what are they just beginning to ask? What might they be asking next year? Five years from now? What do they not even know they don't know yet?

Now look at where those three circles overlap. The sweet spot for YOUR book is where your expertise meets your customers' needs as both they and you look towards the future.

Over to you

- Use the Venn diagram model to identify the 'sweet spot' for your book.
- Identify at least 10 titles you could write in that space.

OR try the next exercise instead.

write the right book – SO What?

Remember good old SWOT analysis? (Yes, I know. Stay with me.)

There's a good reason why plotting your Strengths, Weaknesses, Opportunities and Threats is a cliché of management consultancy: it's an incredibly powerful tool. In case you haven't heard of it (seriously, where have you *been* for the last 40 years?) here it is…

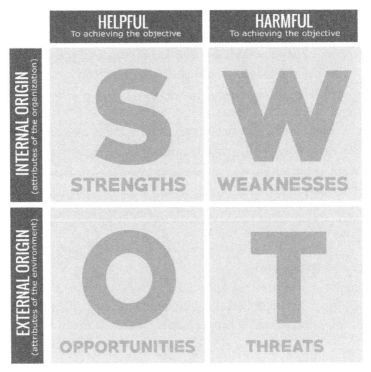

SWOT analysis

(Note that strengths and weaknesses are internal, to do with you and your business, and opportunities and threats are external, to do with what's happening in the wider world.)

STRENGTHS: these are your unique levers of competitive advantage, and should form part of your **positioning statement**. It can be hard to identify your own strengths, so maybe ask someone you trust, or use an online strengths questionnaire such as the VIA survey.[4]

WEAKNESSES: it's very unfashionable these days to talk about weaknesses, but you need to recognize the areas in which you are LESS strong so you can pull together a plan to deal with them. If you're disorganized, get a VA. If you're technically challenged, ensure you have an IT support contract or cultivate a techie friend with a quid pro quo arrangement.

OPPORTUNITIES: these are effectively options for your strategic development, and you can't pursue them all simultaneously. So it's not enough just to recognize them, you also need to prioritize: which is the most compelling? Each opportunity you choose needs to work from a commercial perspective, of course, but it must also be aligned with your deepest values and fit with your unique style, circumstances and personality. Most powerful of all are those opportunities that complement your strengths and are less reliant on areas in which you are weaker.

THREATS: it may be that rather than planning to neutralize these external challenges, the best you can do is

---

[4] http://www.viacharacter.org/www/Character-Strengths-Survey

mitigate against them. But either way, you need to not only recognize them but design your business in full awareness of them, for example by diversifying your portfolio of products, expanding your customer base, or taking out insurance. Think too about competitors, and how you will differentiate yourself.

See, you'd forgotten what a useful wee tool it is, hadn't you?

But what does this have to do with title selection? Allow me to introduce my SO What model (**S**trengths & **O**pportunities – see what I did there?). Once you've done a SWOT analysis you've got a much clearer sense of the best opportunities out there and the strengths at your disposal. So here's the question: does the book you're planning make the most of both? The sweet spot for your book is where those two overlap, where what you do best plays forward into a space that's opening up.

Tim Ferriss did it with *The 4-Hour Work Week*, wedding his own experience with the emerging hunger for the laptop lifestyle. Then he did it again, seeing an opportunity to spin out the success of that concept into the hot topics of health and food with *The 4-Hour Body* and *The 4-Hour Chef* respectively. Brant Cooper and Patrick Vlaskovits did it with *The Lean Entrepreneur*, combining their practical start-up experience and training skills with the revolution in business thinking created by Eric Ries's *The Lean Startup* (which itself took as its starting point Ries's entrepreneurial experience plus the development of lean manufacturing processes).

If you're still undecided about the book you want to write, this is a great opportunity to do some brainstorming; what *could* you write, if you were to marry your unique strengths with the most exciting opportunities you see out there?

When you have a handful of possible titles, that's when you need some prioritization techniques: see the next two chapters.

Over to you

- Use the SO What? tool to identify the 'sweet spot' for your book.
- Identify at least 10 titles you could write in that space.

OR try the previous exercise instead.

---

write the right book – priority quadrants

Once you've done at least one of the exercises above, you will have a list of possible titles, all of which play to your strengths, focus on your target market, and exploit the opportunities available to you. So how do you choose which to pursue first?

You could just pick the one that most appeals to you – and often that's what you'll end up doing anyway! – but it's good to think about it rationally too. As my grandma used to say, you can do anything but you can't do everything. Writing a book takes a huge amount of your most precious resources: your time and your attention. And if you're doing this to build your business, rather than as a passion project, you need to make a decision based on ROI (return on investment).

In agile software development the team must decide which items or features from the backlog to prioritize for inclusion in each short development 'sprint'. The discipline has produced a number of lightweight, effective tools to help in that prioritization process, which you as a business book writer can usefully borrow.

One of the simplest is the priority quadrants matrix, which maps all the possible projects or features you're considering against two axes – the likely positive impact on the business vs the level of effort required. This works perfectly for evaluating book ideas too: the title(s) to pursue first are those in quadrant 1 – these give the highest ROI, or in other words the biggest bang for the lowest buck.

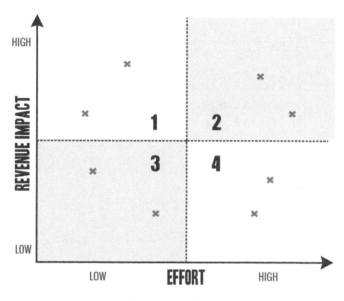

Priority quadrants

But it needn't stop there: it's worth considering what you do with ideas in quadrants 2 and 3. Quadrant 2 represents quick wins: maybe these could be developed into new products, talks, blog posts, free ebooks? And quadrant 3 represents possible new directions: ideas here will take time and headspace, but may be worth investigating as a side hustle alongside the day job.

And Quadrant 4? This is effectively the graveyard of ideas. Leave them for some other sucker.

Over to you

- Map the title ideas you came up with from the previous exercises onto the priority quadrants matrix. Which looks most promising?
- Are there any quick wins or interesting ideas you want to explore in quadrants 2 and 3?

OR try the following exercise instead.

write the right book – decision grid

If priority quadrants are too blunt a tool for you, try constructing a personalized decision grid.

Begin by identifying the key success factors for your book: what do you most want it to achieve for you? How will you measure its success? Create a grid that sets out down one axis all the titles in contention, and along the other these key success factors. Here's a simple example:

	quick to write	fit with target client	fit with planned business activities	potential to build network strategically	TOTAL
title 1	3	9	9	5	26
title 2	9	5	3	2	19
title 3	**7**	**9**	**9**	**8**	**33**
title 4	4	2	2	6	14

Decision grid

Then simply score each potential title against each of those criteria. The obvious winner will be the one with the highest score, but it might be more complicated than that if some of the criteria are more important than others: one of my clients took this very seriously and created an elaborate spreadsheet with weighted criteria. I suspect he engineered the weighting to produce the answer he secretly wanted – and that's fine. You can do all the rational evaluation you like: sometimes you just have a gut preference and you go with it. But at least you'll do so with your eyes open if you've done this work.

Over to you

- Identify what's most important to you about the book you want to write: what do you want it to achieve for your business?
- What will have to happen for you to feel it's been successful?
- Create a decision grid and score the titles you're considering writing against those criteria.

OR try the previous exercise instead.

position yourself

Once you're clear on your business strategy, your target market and the book you're going to write, the positioning statement is a classic tool to bring it all together. It's particularly helpful towards the end of the strategic thinking piece, as you prepare to move over into content marketing and more specifically into writing your book. One reason I love it is that it transforms everything you've learned so far into a form that you can use in your business immediately – which is very much what this book is all about.

A positioning statement is the pure distilled essence of your strategy – who you serve, what makes you different and why it matters – from which all your marketing content (and ultimately your book) will flow. It's deceptively simple, only one or two sentences, but done right it has two big benefits: it forces you to get crystal clear on what makes your business distinctive, and then it helps you communicate that to the world.

So how do you create a positioning statement? Start by brainstorming answers to these questions:

1. Who are you?
2. What is your business?
3. Who is your ideal customer?
4. What are the needs of your ideal customer?
5. Who are your competitors?
6. What is the key benefit of your company over your competitors?
7. What is the unique benefit you offer?

Then spend some time ruthlessly chopping and honing until you've distilled it into the simplest, most powerful expression of your business that you can.

If it helps, you can use a template such as this:

For [target customers] who [have the following problem] I offer [describe the solution] that provides [describe the key benefit]. Unlike [cite the competition], I [describe the key point of competitive differentiation].

The classic positioning statement was that used by Amazon back in 2001 to explain its then-radical business model:

> *For World Wide Web users who enjoy books, Amazon.com is a retail bookseller that provides instant access to over 1.1 million books. Unlike traditional book retailers, Amazon.com provides a combination of extraordinary convenience, low prices, and comprehensive selection.*

Try it out in conversation: do people 'get it'? Are you comfortable saying it? Once you're happy with your positioning statement, use it, or a less formulaic version of it, in your marketing and your networking. Review it regularly to make sure it continues to reflect your business as you evolve. Test your book against it as you write: does the book have the same focus and clarity, and does it fit your ambitions as a business, not just as an author?

Once you're really clear on who you're serving and what you're doing for them, ensure that the book you're writing builds squarely on that. Ghostwriter Ginny Carter calls this 'streamlining' – 'align[ing] your business audience that you already have, that you already market to, with your book audience' – and it makes for a massively more efficient writing and marketing process.

Over to you

- Use that template to create a positioning statement for your business, incorporating all the insights you gained from your work on the 20-year vision and your ideal client/reader.
- How can you use this in your business? How does your chosen book idea fit against it?

The Curve

One of the key questions to ask yourself before you start writing your book is how it will fit into your Curve. You know about The Curve, even if you don't use that word (which was coined by Nicholas Lovell in his book *The Curve: Turning followers into superfans*). You've noticed how successful businesses have been developing offerings at a wide variety of price points, and how they've been focusing particularly on giving stuff away in order to get people's attention and engagement. You probably do it yourself – it's the entire principle behind content marketing, in fact. But have you thought strategically about how and where your book fits in?

Here's how Nicholas Lovell explained it when I spoke to him:

> 'The Curve comes in three parts. You have to find an audience. That probably, but doesn't necessarily, involve free. You have to earn the right to talk to them again. It's no good having a newsletter that you get people to sign up for if they immediately unsubscribe because your content is boring and rubbish. Then, having done those two things, found them and got the right to talk to them again, you have to let those people who really want to spend money with you, the people who love what you do, the superfans, spend lots of money on things they really value.'

I use this model with clients regularly now, and I've noticed some interesting ways their Curve can fail them:

1. **It stops prematurely**. Often, people don't have any way that superfans can spend serious money with them. So you have a free webinar, a newsletter, maybe an online course, workshops and some one-to-one client work. That's great. But what do you do when your one-to-one clients want more? How can you create products and services that your superfans will value so much they're prepared to pay prices that make you blush? You only need to sell one VIP package a year to make that sort of deal worthwhile. And if you sell four or five, you might just have transformed your business at a stroke.

2. **It has gaps**. If there's no offering between the book and the top-rate bespoke consultancy, you'll lose most of your interested-but-not-committed potential clients. People need time to get to know and trust you. It can take years – literally – for some clients to move their way step by step along The Curve, gaining confidence and trust at each step.

3. **It isn't smooth**. Your job, as Nicholas Lovell puts it, is to move people along The Curve. 'If you want more, here's how to get it.' At each step some people will be satisfied (for now at least) and pause, others will want more. Make it as easy as possible for them to know what the next step is and take it, ideally in a single click.

Your book probably isn't free, so it's a little way along The Curve, but you can create a free taster to drive people up to it. The obvious thing is to put up a sample chapter, but that's a pretty unsatisfying experience for a reader, as you'll know if you've ever tried it yourself. As Lovell puts it: 'the free thing should be a whole experience or a whole useful thing that is free.' His solution was to create a free short ebook, *10 Ways to Make Money in a Free World*, which summarizes the principles of The Curve and gives 10 practical ideas for implementing it. (The additional benefit is that this neatly exploits Amazon's algorithms – everyone who downloads this book sees *The Curve* top of the 'Customers Who Bought This Item Also Bought' list.)

And once someone's bought the book, what then? What's the next logical step for your reader on YOUR business's Curve? Your potential superfans will finish your book and say to themselves, 'That was great! Now what?' Your job is to give them a clear answer.[5]

Over to you

- Draw out The Curve of your business. Does it go far enough? Are there gaps? Is it a smooth progression? If not, how can you improve it?
- What's the next step along The Curve for your readers when they finish your book?

---

[5] As I make clear in the Introduction and at the end, the next step after reading this book is to join The Extraordinary Business Book Club for regular insights and inspiration. No harm repeating it here.

try the buy button test

If you *really* want to know if your book or indeed business idea has legs, the best way isn't to ask people, it's to see if they buy it.

I've done market research. I've gone out and talked to people and asked, 'Would you like this product? Would you buy this product?' And most people, perhaps because they're polite and feel bad about saying 'No' to my face, or maybe because they're infected by my enthusiasm and genuinely mean it in the moment, say 'Yes, I would absolutely buy that product.'

They might, or they might not. (They probably won't.)

Measuring those who actually click through to spend real money on a product is a much more reliable indicator, and you can use it even if you don't actually have a product to sell yet.

Nicholas Lovell had an idea for a new gaming book, *The F2P [Free to Play] Toolbox.*

'I wanted to test as quickly and cheaply as possible whether or not there was going to be a market for this book. I just put an ad up on my website. The ad said...
"Buy it now!" And if you clicked on the ad it took you to a page that said, "Look, I'm really sorry, but I haven't written this book yet. I was running a test to see whether or not people were interested. If enough of you show you are interested by clicking, then I'll go ahead and write it. If you want me to write it, why don't you give me your email address now and I'll email you when it's ready?" I got 150 emails within a couple of weeks, which was enough to make me think there's a market and a revenue opportunity for me here.'

The book, which he self-published, had made around £50,000 when we spoke, so I guess he was right.

This takes chutzpah, and you need to craft a good message for those who click through only to find the book is not yet written, but if you're debating whether it's worthwhile writing a particular book – or even creating a particular product – it's a great way of testing the market's appetite. And you could even enlist these early enthusiasts in the process of writing, to **build your street team** right up front.

Over to you

Do you want to test whether there's a market for your book, and whether you could sell it direct? If so, this might be a technique to consider. Ask yourself:

- How quickly could I deliver the book if there's a good response?
- Do I have the infrastructure in place to sell direct when the book's published?
- What's my message for those who click through before it's ready?
- What level of response would suggest this is a viable idea, and how long will I give it?
- If there's a good response, how could I use those who click through in the process of writing?
- If there's a poor response, what's my plan for responding to those who click through?

micro-niche and customize

Print-on-demand technology has opened up new possibilities for business book writers. You can now create bespoke versions of your book in small quantities relatively quickly and cheaply.

One way to use this is to repurpose your book to fit a micro-niche. Michael E. Gerber did this with his E-Myth series and so did Warren Knight with *Think #Digital First*; in both cases they wrote the original book for a well-defined but fairly broad audience, then created versions tailored to very specific industries.

Michael E. Gerber collaborated with experts in each industry: the E-Myth material remained relatively unchanged each time, but he chose a co-author from each sector – real estate, accountancy, etc – to draw out the specific application of his methodology for that field.

Warren Knight sold the concept of the niched version of *Think #Digital First* with the aid of a mock-up:

'I literally just turned up with a printout: this is going to be the book cover and these are the chapters, and instead of saying 'entrepreneur', we're going to say 'a jewellery business'. And they went, "Oh, God, that's amazing. We love that, Warren. No problem at all, we'll get you speaking, we'll do this, we'll do that, we'll take the books," and so I knew, before I'd even started, that there was a potential opportunity for me there. So my very first one was in the jewellery industry. I then went into the giftware industry, the beauty industry, the fitness industry, the hearing aid industry... It was

great because it was all about personalization and relevance to that audience.'

Another possibility is customization for a specific customer: one of my authors offers her corporate clients the option of having a foreword from the CEO and an appendix of company-specific contact details added to her book when they do a bulk purchase.

Over to you

- Is there an opportunity for you to micro-niche or customize your book for a specific audience?
- If so, why not find a potential collaborator or customer and discuss what that might look like, and what opportunities it might open up?

GROWING YOUR PLATFORM

'When you're selling, really, anything, these days... you've got to have these trust touchpoints with people... they read a piece of content that was valuable, or they saw a tweet that you shared, that they thought was great, or you met in person, they saw you speak, or just as simple as maybe they walked by your book. Any time you can do things like that, that engage them at certain moments, you start going from their short term to long term memory in a way that's positive, and it's positioned correctly. Then, they think of you at the right moment, when they need something in your space.' – John Hall, Influence & Co

As John Hall makes clear, it's not enough just to publish a book if you want to be top of mind with potential customers. And sadly it's not enough just to publish a good book to have people buy and read it. People need a reason to read, and that means they need a way of hooking your book into what they already know and care about. If you're lucky, they're actively looking for books on this topic and stumble across you on Amazon. More likely they won't even notice your book unless they've already heard of you. And that's where your platform comes in.

Adrian Zackheim, founder of Portfolio, Penguin's prestigious business book list, knows a thing or two about acquiring and marketing business books. An existing platform – a strong social media following, highly ranked blog, YouTube channel, podcast or the like – is a key factor when he's making acquisition decisions.

'When we're taking on an author who has never had a book published before, one of the indications that this is a person we should consider is the pre-existence of a significant platform... because that means that this person has already started to attract a community, and that that community can be built upon. It's an obvious strategy for publishers to seek out people with pre-existing platforms and attempt to extend them.'

(There's an awkward Catch-22 for traditional publishers here, of course: if someone has a strong platform, they may feel they don't need a traditional publisher at all.)

But his logic is irrefutable. You may have needed a gatekeeper such as a publisher or broadcaster 10 years ago to get your ideas out and build some energy around them: now you have an embarrassment of channels and tools through which and with which to disseminate them. If you're not using them, why not?

As you grow your own platform you'll discover an ironic side benefit: other people are more willing to promote you on THEIR platform once you have your own. It's partly social proof, partly reciprocity. The result is that the work you put into your platform development has an exponential impact on your visibility.

It all starts here.

start with the platform, not the book

Kelly Pietrangeli has two young sons. Like many working mums she lived in a perpetual state of overwhelm, feeling out of control of her life. Unlike most, however, Kelly did something about it: she went on parenting and productivity courses, and then formed a mutual coaching circle with a small group of friends to keep herself on track. It worked brilliantly, and after a couple of years they said to each other, 'We should write a book.'

So they started writing a book, until Kelly had a revelation.

'It just occurred to me one day, how are we going to get a book deal... when we have no website, no social media platform whatsoever, like, who are we, you know? We're just a couple of mothers who are writing this book, and I suddenly lost confidence in the idea. But then it occurred to me, well, we could kind of do things backwards here and set up a website, and take the chapters we've written so far and turn them into blog posts.'

Her friend and co-author wasn't impressed.

'What, we're just going to take all this stuff we've been working on and just put it for free on a website so anybody can get it? Why would anybody later want to buy a book if it's already there on the website?'

But Kelly convinced her and Project Me was born, first as a blog, then gradually as a suite of resources, online courses, workshops and ultimately a community.

And it was that community that turned things around when it was time to circle back and write the book.

'I was able to take all of those wonderful things that people wrote and put them in the book proposal saying at the end of it, "And here is what my readers are saying about wanting to have this book." I basically quoted everybody… so the publishers were able to see that I've already built my tribe. I've already got this following and they're following every step of the way on this book writing.'

The result? She put aside the pitch she'd prepared for the meeting with publishers when she realized they were pitching to *her* in a bidding war.

What Kelly discovered is that a book is part of your bigger platform, not a standalone. To get readers, let alone publishers, interested in your book to the point where they're willing to spend time and money on it, you have to secure their attention. And to make the book worthwhile for you professionally, there has to be a 'back-end' of revenue-creating activities that the book can point people towards.

Before you think about writing your book, think about creating a platform – content, products, services, community. And ideally, like Kelly, create the two together, to maximize the return on your investment.

Over to you

- Draw a map of where your book sits within your wider platform.
- Where are you making opportunities to get your ideas out into the world?
- How can those online and offline touchpoints work to reinforce each other?

plan your content strategy

Why content matters

Being in business today means creating content. Google rewards long posts and frequent updates, the half-life of a tweet is measured in minutes, and the range of channels and volume of competing information is enough to make you weep.

Creating quality, engaging, shareable material can feel like an endless, thankless chore: how often should you blog? Do you email your list at least once a week? Got your own YouTube channel? Scheduled your tweets today?

But it's an essential chore. Very few people are prepared to pay for online content, but it's the price by which businesses purchase attention, and without attention there is no sale. Dorie Clark put it beautifully:

'As a journalist I used to get paid to write articles. That was the definition of my job. But nowadays I spend plenty of time writing articles and yet I don't get paid for it at all... I actually make far more money now than I did when I was a journalist but the way that I have been able to do that is to monetize around the journalism. You write an article. Well, you might get zero for the article but if you've placed it in the right venue you may get a $15,000 or $20,000 speech out of that article. You might get a consulting contract. You might get access to opportunities that you couldn't even have predicted.

*You have to really open yourself up in the words of the internet theorist Doc Searls away from making money **from** something and understand that nowadays you make money **because of** something and that's a very different phenomenon.'*

Your content makes you discoverable online and it allows potential clients to build a relationship with you before they've even met you: they read what you write and they learn to like and trust you, which is a basic prerequisite for spending money with you. People buy people, and in the online world people get to know people by the content they're putting out there.

How writing a book can help

So you might think, sheesh, if I already have to create more content than I can cope with, I must be nuts to take on writing a book AS WELL. But here's the clever bit: when you use the writing of your book as the engine of your content strategy, it's a double win.

You could sit in a room and write every word of your book in a Word document, like dropping pennies in a piggy bank – put in a penny every day for 100 days and you'll have a pound, and you can go out and buy something. Churn out 500 words every day for 100 days and, look, a 50,000-word book. But none of those words would have done you any good while it was sitting around waiting for the others.

But if you write your book as a sequence of content outputs that you can put out there right from the start you begin to see a return on your investment up front. Plan it right, and the process of writing your book can provide you with a content strategy for the next six months or more, and help you build the platform from which you'll launch the book along the way. You'll also get feedback on your ideas and the way in which you're expressing them, which never hurts.

Creating a content plan

There are lots of ways to plan your content – the CMI has a particularly useful one-page template.[6] But basically, just like your book, it all starts with what you're trying to achieve in your business.

When I help clients plan a content strategy we start with their **working table of contents** and triangulate that against their business activities over the next six months or so. (If there's no obvious match, that's a red flag and we'll go back and look again at how the book fits with the business.) We then work out how they can use sections of the book to support each activity.

So for example if you're giving a talk at a networking event in a month's time, can you use that to outline your introduction, mapping out the big ideas and making the case for the change you want to see in the world? If you're about to launch a new workshop, can you create handouts that you can use as resources for the book? If you're promoting a product, can you write a series of blog posts

---

[6] http://contentmarketinginstitute.com/2017/04/content-strategy-one-page-plan/

based around client stories you're collecting for the book? If you're wanting to increase your visibility in a particular area, can you draft a chapter of the book and pitch it as a guest article for a publication with great reach in that field?

There's a checklist of content outputs at the end of this book to give you some ideas but it's by no means exhaustive.

Over to you

- Identify at least five bits of content you could create based on what you're writing for your book: blog posts, talk outlines, webinars, vlogs/ videos, client case studies, whatever. (Don't forget they don't have to be one-off pieces: you can create a blog or YouTube series, an 8-week course – whatever works best for you.)
- When will you put them out and how will you use them to build the business?

take a content audit

It's worth taking some time to think about what you already have before you start writing your book from the ground up. Use this one with caution: it's easy to think that because you have 26 hours of audio material, a 6-week online course or three years of weekly blogging behind you that all you have to do is pull it all together, insert chapter headings, and get it typeset. That might work if you started blogging as a way of writing the book in the first place, but otherwise it's likely to produce a jumbled mess.

We've all read books like that – and usually they're disappointing experiences. (The exceptions are where the articles are substantial and well-written in the first place and carefully selected, more like a collection of essays.)

Your old content reflects the journey that got you here, which is great, but your book is a tool for the future. Better to start from where you are now, using the tools in **Growing your business**. But once you're clear who you're writing for and what your message is, it makes sense to look at what you've already created and see if there's anything that might have a place in your book.

One way to do this is to take a content audit, as big companies do when they're tidying up corporate websites or intranets, but it's a useful principle for wider application too. The basic steps are these:

1. Create an inventory.
2. Classify the content.
3. Establish what (if anything) to do with it.

Spend a couple of hours identifying all the significant bits of original content you've created over the last two years or so. You can create a spreadsheet listing each piece with a hyperlink to its location (online or on your computer). Make sure file names are helpful; not blog.doc but something more meaningful, e.g. 'content audit blog.doc'.

As you create your inventory, think about the metadata you want to capture. You might want to add a column for 'type', for example, so you can identify whether this is a blog post, a guest article, a podcast transcript, a training script, whatever. It would be useful to add the date it was created, and maybe an estimate of the number of words. And you can also classify it: the list of tags on your blog is a good starting point for this and provides a consistent, controlled vocabulary. What's the main topic (or main two or three topics, if you must) for each piece?

And finally, take your **working table of contents** and assess whether each piece might have a place in the book you're planning to write. You could drop the entire article in under the appropriate heading as a placeholder to revise later, or just take a paragraph or two as a starting point.

I used this technique extensively in the writing of this book – I drafted the original table of contents in Excel with links to relevant posts. In a few cases the blogs I'd written off the back of podcast interviews went in pretty much unchanged, but most of the time they provided a jumping-off point for a rewritten version.

To make this an even more valuable exercise, benefiting your wider platform and not just your book, identify the articles/posts you're most proud of and which are continuing to perform well in terms of traffic, shares, likes and/or inbound links. In publishing terms this is called the 'backlist': the stuff published a while back, but which is still valuable and interesting to someone happening upon it for the first time. It's where most publishers make their steady money, often over many years. Schedule regular social media links pointing people to archive material alongside links to the new stuff and you've just doubled your content marketing impact at a stroke. When I did this for the Extraordinary Business Book Club podcast the listening figures doubled almost overnight.

As well as simply pointing people to backlist content, you can also consider updating or reworking your best-performing posts. Again, in publishing terms, this is like a commissioning editor noticing that a high-performing title is ready for a new edition. Keep the original URL (you don't want to mess up all those links) and add a note to explain what's going on: 'This article was originally written in April 2017 and updated in November 2018,' for example.

If you spot a good post that hasn't performed as well as you think it should have, think about changing the title, adding keyword tags or a different image and share it again: everyone deserves a second chance. And if you spot a post that's embarrassingly outdated you can quietly delete it.

Over to you

Set aside some time to do a content audit.

- What do you discover about what you've already created?
- How can you use the best, most relevant material in your book?
- Which material deserves to be promoted more widely and which needs to be updated?

write your biography

When you step onto a platform to present your ideas to the world, having a good answer to the question 'Who are you, anyway?' is essential. It's also a vital part of writing a book. You'll need a strong biography for a proposal (if you're submitting one) and for marketing materials. In any case it's a great exercise to make you focus on what it is about you that's distinctive and engaging to readers, so you might as well get it done sooner rather than later.

I run a regular 10-day Business Book Proposal Challenge, working through every field of the book proposal template with a group of would-be authors. Day 5, author biography day, is the one many find the hardest. It's like writing your CV for that big job: how to come across as confident and credible without sounding cocky? How do you know which bits to focus on and what to leave out?

There are two kinds of credentials these days – formal and social – and their relative importance and the balance between them will depend on the kind of book you're writing.

Formal credentials include obvious things like qualifications: your Masters in Psychology or your honorary doctorate, and any published research you've done. They also include relevant industry experience and positions, including your professional experience and notable jobs, and also wider roles such as chairing a trade organization or contributing to an industry publication. What's great about those sorts of credentials is they not only demonstrate you know what you're talking about, they suggest that you're well connected and well respected in the area, so use them for all they're worth. If you're writing a book for students or professionals, strong formal credentials are vital.

However **social credentials** are becoming more and more important so, no matter how good your formal credentials are, you need to pay them some attention. And if your formal credentials are weak this is where you have to shine. If you can show me that other people are listening to you, that you've already moved the needle, then I'm more likely to believe that you're worth listening to.

So how do you evidence those social credentials in your biography? Here's some ideas:

- Endorsements: what well-known/respected people in the field say about you
- Speaking engagements
- Workshops or seminars that you've led
- Your own blog
- Popular blogs or publications, for which you've written
- Your own podcast or podcasts that you've appeared on as a guest
- Your YouTube channel
- A large and engaged email list
- A popular Facebook page or group
- A strong following on other social media channels such as Twitter or Instagram.

Choose the ones that are strongest for you, obviously, but make sure they're relevant: there's no point having 10,000 active followers as a mummy blogger if you're writing a book about financial planning.

Depending on the book, your own personal story can be one of the most important parts of your biography: the fact that you were an alcoholic and you're writing about recovery is obviously important, for example. But if you're telling your own story be disciplined: focus on the relevant details and don't be tempted to give the world a full autobiography. Literally nobody cares where you went to school. Sorry.

Finally, think about your contacts because if your own credentials are weak, these can save the day. If you haven't got a Facebook profile but you're best friends with Oprah, the world will probably still listen to you.

(I wish it wasn't this way, truly. I wish you could just write a really good book and have readers recognize its quality and fall over themselves to read it, but that isn't the world we live in any more. Maybe it never was.)

As you already know, though, the good news is that if your biography looks a bit weedy right now that's OK, because you can use the writing of your book to build your platform and beef it up.

Over to you

- Write your biography as you'd like it to appear in your book (keep it honest!). Extra points if you can keep it under 250 words, but it shouldn't be longer than 400.
- Reflect on what you've discovered: how can you use that biography in your business? What weren't you making the most of before? What do you need to work on in future? Was there discomfort and if so what does that tell you?

start blogging

One of the themes that keeps coming up in the Extraordinary Business Book Club is the importance of blogging. Seth Godin is particularly passionate and persuasive:

> '*Blogging is a privilege, and even if no one reads your blog, you should have one... It requires you to put your name on the thought. It requires you to predict something that's going to happen, or explain something that has happened. It leaves a trail. If you know that every day, day after day, 365 days a year, you are going to be leaving a trail, a trail about ideas, about culture, about the work you think that matters, I can't help but imagine that you will think about it a little more deeply. You will think about it subconsciously. You will dream about it. It will be on the agenda every single day. That is a wonderful gift to the blogger, regardless of whether anyone reads it or not...*
>
> *Then the other half of it, which is very significant, is that we live in an economy that is based on connection and gifts. Not on scarcity, but abundance. Ideas don't travel under the same rules as most things in economics. Economics, from the Greek for 'scarce'. What we have to realize is that if I have an idea and I share it with you, it's not worth less. It's worth more.*'

I was so inspired by this that I committed to blog daily after that conversation with Seth, and guess what? He's right. (See **streaking**.)

But even if you don't blog every day, blogging is a great tool for business book authors. Here's why:

1. It gets you into the writing habit and that makes you a better writer and (the evidence suggests) more successful all round. Productivity expert Bec Evans says:

   'We often think of "prolific" as a bit of a dirty word but fundamentally the more you write the better you get. If you apply that in a deliberate way and learn from it you will become a better writer. Be prolific in your volume, be prolific in your writing habit, writing every single day, and having lots and lots of ideas. You really don't know which of your ideas are going to work until you've put them out into the world.'

2. It helps you get found. Publicist Ben Cameron made this point strongly:

   '[Blogging] helps you in so many ways – it sets you up as an expert, it helps your search engine optimization, so people can find you. It helps people find your business as well as giving you a opportunity to tell people about your book when it comes out... it helps people find you when they type into Google, "I'm looking for a business that does this."'

   (Google's algorithms are mysterious in many ways but they consistently favour sites that feature regular, high-quality, consistent new content with inbound and outbound links.)

3. It builds your network. Brant Cooper, author of *The Lean Entrepreneur*, blogged about the frustration of not being able to get funding behind his early attempts at implementing lean principles in sales and marketing. One of his readers put him in touch with Steve Blank, who became pivotal in the Lean Entrepreneurship movement.

4. It allows you to test out ideas and terminology. One of my clients, Joanna, used a blog post to test out a metaphor she was toying with for her book: the flurry of 'OMG YES!!' comments and shares told her she'd nailed it.

5. Finally, it's a vehicle for you to start putting out there sections of your book as you write it and to build interest and engagement. Your blog followers will become your book champions and it takes time and consistency to build that following.

Where should you blog? Ideally on your own site – any website platform worth the name will have a blog function. These are your thoughts and they should first and foremost furnish the corner of the internet that you own.

But don't leave them there: share your blog far and wide through social media. Include guest posts on other sites or LinkedIn and link to and from them. Very few people will come to your site to read that marketing copy you crafted so carefully, but share a link to a blog post on something they care about and suddenly you have their attention.

Don't forget other people's blogs too: leaving a thoughtful comment on a relevant high-profile blogger's site is a good way of bringing people back to your site. Once you're blogging, you're part of a bigger conversation.

Over to you

If you're already blogging consistently, move along to **blog smarter**.

If you're not blogging consistently, ask yourself:

- What will I blog about? (Hint: start with your **working table of contents**!)
- How often can I commit to blogging? (For some thoughts on the benefits of daily blogging, see **streaking**.)
- What channels and platforms will I use to host and share blog posts?

blog smarter

Once you're blogging regularly, it's time to start blogging smarter.

Here are a few advanced blogging strategies specifically aimed at business book writers:

1. **Think visually.** The web is a visual place and a striking image is more likely to catch the eye of anyone scrolling through their social media feed. At the very least associate a 'featured image' with each blog post, and use meaningful 'alt' text and description to help with discovery. (NB as with your book, make sure you're using royalty-free images and credit attribution if necessary – just because it's on the internet doesn't mean it's not copyright material!) You can create unique images including the title of your blog and your branding very quickly and easily using free tools such as Canva or Stencil. Or take it a step further and create infographics or diagrams that not only help you think through and present your topic in a different way but which can be used or adapted as book illustrations.

2. **Use topic categories.** Pretty much every blogging platform allows you to assign categories to posts, and you can use these as the key planks of your content strategy, including your book. Identify the big topics you want to write about – these may match up with the chapters in your book – and use these as your key categories, assigning each blog post to at least one. This will help people discover

your content more easily and also guide them to other posts in the same area.

3. **Use type categories**. As well as thinking of blog posts in terms of topic categories, you can categorize them by type. Here are a few examples of type categories used by my clients: 'how-tos', 'deep dives', 'weekly challenge', 'case study', 'interview', 'top 10', 'infographics', 'reviews', 'resources'. They use these type categories to plan their content strategy and give a structure and consistency to their output. Even if you're not using this technique fully you can create type categories for your own purposes: all the blog posts I wrote for this book were tagged 'TBMB' on my blog so that I could identify them easily.

4. **Add a call to action**. So many great blog posts simply end at the end. If a reader's read this far they obviously like what you're saying, so why not give them a next step? When you're writing a book you have an ace up your sleeve: rather than asking people to sign up so you can sell at them, you can invite your readers to get involved by sending you their stories or ideas. As your writing progresses, you can invite them to become part of your **street team** or even **beta readers**. When the blog ends, the relationship is just beginning.

5. **Keep promoting the good stuff**. Some blog posts are of the moment and that's fine. But when you really invest time and energy in creating an evergreen post with great content and a long shelf life (like the kind of stuff you're going to be writing for inclusion in a book, say), don't let it fall into

internet oblivion after a couple of days. Use social media scheduling software such as HootSuite, eClincher or Sprout Social to schedule regular links to posts 'from the archive'. You can add a note at the end if necessary to update the post with your latest thinking on an issue.

Over to you

- Choose one of these advanced techniques.
- Plan how to implement it on your blog this week.

build your email list

Content marketing and social media are great ways to engage attention, but you need a way to convert that into a relationship if you're to generate revenue from it, and that happens through your email list.

A healthy email list is the lifeblood of businesses in the internet age and your book provides multiple opportunities to build it: as you write, at launch, and for years afterwards.

There are three basic steps to a successful list strategy:

1. Attract the right people to sign up.
2. Keep them signed up.
3. Use the list right.

Attract the right people to sign up

Don't get sucked into the numbers game. Whether your list is 10, 100, 1,000 or 10,000+, what really matters is who those people are and how engaged they are. Much better to have 100 people squarely in your target market who read your stuff than 10,000 random souls who auto-delete it.

And that means setting the right bait: what 'lead magnet' or freebie could you create to incentivize your dream customer to sign up to your list? ('Sign up to my newsletter' on its own doesn't have much pulling power, sorry.) My strongest lead magnet is my 10-day Business Book Proposal Challenge, closely followed by the Kickstart Workbook: both deliver real value to the people I most want to reach, those at the early stages of planning a book to build their business.

Keep them signed up

Once someone has signed up to your list they've effectively agreed to go on a date with you. They're not ready for a proposal yet; they hardly know you. So every email you send has to reflect how you'd like to come across on a first date: be yourself, sure, but be your best self. It's appropriate to promote your stuff in your emails, but the ratio needs to be firmly weighted towards useful/ entertaining content if you're to keep your subscribers.

There will always be unsubscribes and that's fine. It doesn't serve you or them if a subscriber with no interest in what you're saying stays on your list out of inertia or a desire not to offend. But if you see a big spike in unsubscribes after a particular email, it's worth reviewing it and seeing if there are lessons to be learned.

Use the list right

As with content marketing, you need to know what the call to action is for any email you send to your list – and ideally keep it to one per email. Think about how you can make your subscribers feel rewarded rather than simply sold to: a discount code or early access, letting them know about a freebie, creating some bonus material etc.

How often you email your list is up to you: I send out a weekly newsletter which takes quite a while to create as it's very content-rich. Consistency, both in how often you email and the quality, tone and structure of the emails you send, is important, so find a timescale that works for you and your readers and stick to it. One of the great benefits of a regular bulletin is that it keeps you top of mind, even if a recipient doesn't even click through to read, and you never know when they're going to be ready to make the decision to buy.

When you add a book into the mix, an email list suddenly gets even more interesting. You can use it to **source stories** or get feedback on ideas or cover designs, you can build interest and engagement by giving them behind-the-scenes access to the writing process, and ultimately invite them to join your **street team**, and you can coordinate them to buy your book at a specific time and date to catapult you to a bestseller slot on launch. As Joanna Penn puts it:

> *'Imagine how powerful it is to have a list of 10,000 people and to send an email saying "My book is available now. Click here to buy." This is the basis of all the Amazon bestseller campaigns.'* [7]

As you get more confident you can do all sorts of fancy advanced tricks with email automation, such as creating trigger emails based on how someone responded to the last email, segmenting your list to target a message more narrowly, creating workflows that take people from one campaign to another based on behaviour. But none of that is a substitute for providing good-quality, useful content to people who want it.

---

[7] www.thecreativepenn.com/2010/09/25/how-authors-and-writers-can-build-an-email-list-for-marketing/

Over to you

- Do you have the plumbing in place to create and grow an email list? At the very least you'll need a freebie offer and a landing page to put it on, with a sign-up form, linked to marketing automation software such as MailChimp or Drip. There are numerous online tutorials, or you can work with a professional (this is a core part of what the digital marketing experts I work with in my This Book Means Business mentorship programme cover).
- What lead magnet can you create for your target market? Think VIP – Valuable, Individual, Professional.

launch a podcast

One of the most wonderful things to have come out of this book journey has been the launching of the Extraordinary Business Book Club podcast. It's hard to remember that it actually started primarily as a way to force me to write this book. There were two key dimensions to that plan:

1. **Accountability**. If I was broadcasting to the world week by week about how I was getting on with my own book, surely I'd have to write it out of sheer embarrassment if nothing else.
2. **Content creation**. I wanted more examples of smart ways to write business-building books: what better way to find them than interviewing successful business book authors?

Both worked beautifully (though the writing took way longer than I'd imagined).

But the podcast has become *so* much more than that and now I recommend it as a top strategy for anyone wanting to build their platform (and, inevitably, their network, their business and themselves too).

Joanna Penn started The Creative Penn podcast back in 2009, before podcasting was even a thing, and she believes it's still one of the best ways to connect with your tribe, IF you can be consistent and stay the course – she agreed to be a guest on my show only after I'd done 15 episodes, because:

'So many people start podcasts but then disappear, so I figure if you can do 15 you're probably committed...

we're at that point with podcasting where we were with blogging in 2008, 2009 probably. Podcasting's now the real way to connect so I think it is very powerful but as with anything, you have to commit for the longer term and then it is very rewarding.'

Here's why podcasting ticks all the platform development boxes for me:

1. **It's easy to do, but most people think it's hard**. If you're going to produce credible YouTube videos you need decent cameras, lights, video editing skills and – the killer for me – you need to scrub up, make up and dress up. Not to mention finding a corner of the house that looks like a TV set. For podcasting? I started with the built-in mic of my MacBook Pro. I use Skype with Call Recorder and Audacity to edit, all free, easy-to-use bits of software. And I can do it in my pyjamas.

2. **It's intrinsically interesting**. Or at least it should be. I use the interview format, and I get to talk to interesting people about my most favourite topics. What's not to like? Interviewing people is a fabulous way to indulge your curiosity and if you're enjoying the conversation and learning things your listeners will be too. And frankly if you don't find it intrinsically interesting and enjoyable, you won't keep it up.

3. **It's niche**. That sounds like it should be a bad thing but one of the most glorious things about podcasts is that you can come at things from an entirely new angle and/or dive deep into the niche of your

choice. No matter how many podcasts are out there (and there are *lots*), you can still find a unique space or approach, and you must. Think long and hard about who you want to reach, what they care about, and what you bring to the party: in the Extraordinary Business Book Club I get authors to talk about the mechanics of how they plumb their book into their business. They've never been asked about that before and that makes it interesting for them as well as for the listeners.

4. **It's user-friendly.** I don't watch many YouTube videos – I don't have time. Videos demand my full attention and my attention is a very scarce commodity. I read a lot, obviously. But I spend a lot of time doing things that preclude both reading and watching videos, such as running and driving, and that's when I turn to podcasts.

5. **It's engaging.** There's something very intimate about listening to someone's voice, much more so than reading the words they've written. I'm more unguarded in a podcast than I would be in a blog. I drop in details about my life, I definitely emote more (in fact once I actually cried laughing during a podcast, thank you Andy Cope). The result is that those who listen to my podcast feel they know me and they've started to like and trust me. And that's a great position from which to start a conversation with a prospective client.

6. **It's growing.** According to the Pew Research Center in 2016,[8] 21% of Americans aged over 12

---

[8] www.journalism.org/2016/06/15/podcasting-fact-sheet/

had listened to a podcast in the previous month, up from 12% in 2013. It's still a minority, but it's growing fast. Digital audio is the big success story of publishing in recent years and as speakers controlled by voice assistants such as Alexa become commonplace in homes, digital audio will only grow in popularity.

7. **It opens up opportunities**. I've interviewed some of my idols over the last year or so and I'm now on the radar of the publicity department of every major publisher of business books. When you host a podcast you own a prime bit of internet real estate. Instead of courting the rockstars as a fan you're offering them a platform, and that's a very different conversation.

8. **It generates top-drawer original content**. The podcast itself is a central part of your content strategy of course, but in addition you can use it as the basis of blogs, courses, videos, articles and so on. And for each of these outputs you can tag your interviewee who will almost certainly share it with his or her followers. Boom.

I absolutely love hosting the Extraordinary Business Book Club (and apparently it shows). I finish each interview feeling electrified and inspired, and each time I re-read the transcripts I notice another gem that I missed first time round. It's brain food of the highest quality and I get to share it with anyone who'll listen.

And here's the thing: I just decided to do it. I had a million reasons not to, and paralysing fear about looking an idiot or messing up the tech, but I decided to do it anyway. I knew I'd enjoy it and I knew it would be good for business, and that was enough.

If you're hovering on the brink, here's a tip that several of my clients have used: create a podcast series on a particular topic, say six interviews. That way you can 'try out' podcasting, see if you enjoy it enough to want to continue, and if it resonates with your audience. If not, you still have six interesting interviews which you can mine for their networking and content value, and which will give you a toe-hold for discovery on audio platforms such as SoundCloud, iTunes and Stitcher. But if you fall in love with it as I did you can create more series and link them together and, before you know it, you're a podcaster, baby.

Over to you

- If you're considering a podcast, draw up a project evaluation: what are the costs (primarily time and opportunity costs), what are the potential benefits (specifically for you and your business), and what are the risks?
- Decide on your approach: what niche will you make your own? Who's it for and what's the hook? How will it relate to your book?

GROWING YOUR NETWORK

Every business exists within a wide range of relationships and it's worth planning how you can use the process of writing your book to build those relationships, and your network, strategically. This starts long before the book is actually published.

Several participants in the 10-day proposal challenge have told me they don't want to talk about their book before it's published because they're terrified someone else will steal the idea. I have two responses to that a) so get the thing written and published sooner rather than later, and b) once you put the idea out there and make it your own you claim it publicly; if someone then steals it and passes it off as their own that's a risk to their reputation. If you wouldn't take that risk, what makes you think your competitors would? (My third answer, which is unpopular, is that ideas are two-a-penny anyway: the magic is in the implementation.)

For my money, the benefits of being open about your book in its early stages massively outweigh the risks. You can crowd-source ideas and examples, carry out research, invite opinions and strengthen your network to build your business. If you're involving your tribe, those who already know and like and trust you, you immediately secure three big benefits:

1. You're far more likely to actually get the thing done if you've made it public.
2. You will build anticipation and awareness of the book so that when it's finally published there's a group of people ready to buy immediately and recommend it to their friends – and the more they've felt involved in its creation, the more true this will be.
3. Finally and quite simply, the more you involve your **target reader**ship in its writing, the better the book will be.

Try out some of these ideas to see how writing your book can build your network – upwards and outwards – from Day 1.

map your network

Before you start planning how best to build your network, it's worth taking some time to understand it better and identify the opportunities.

Here's one useful model: you might want to replace one or more of the labels in the outer circles with ones more meaningful for you.

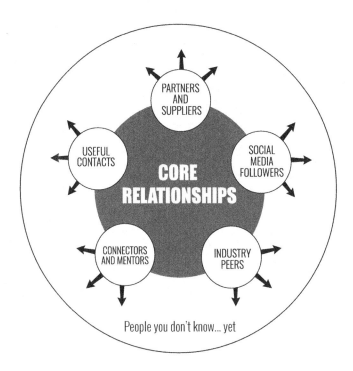

Network map

Identify your main network clusters: your core (e.g. existing clients, Facebook group etc) and related groups (e.g. JV partners, suppliers, social media followers etc).

Within each group, identify key individuals likely to be interested in your book and think about who else they could connect you with.

Here are a few examples to get you started:

1. **Local networking group**: offer to speak on a topic included in the book; ask for recommendations for other speaking gigs.
2. **Target clients**: identify key contacts and email them to suggest featuring them as a case study
3. **Rockstars**: ask for a quote on the topic or even an interview for research.

And remember that your network doesn't stop with your immediate connections: each of the people you know will know someone else who could be just the person you need to connect with as you write. Don't be shy of asking for connections.

Patrick McGinnis, author of *The 10% Entrepreneur*, shared a tip that I now use shamelessly in the Extraordinary Business Book Club podcast:

'Every time I would talk to somebody, I did the old interview question trick, the old "can you tell me three people you know who are doing this" sort of thing.'

Here's why it works so well:

1. **It takes me beyond my own existing network.** That was plenty big enough to get me started, but when you're putting out a weekly show you quickly need to bring in new ideas and new voices.

2. **It takes me beyond the obvious**. I'd never have thought of the connection between writing a business book and UX expertise if Giles Colborne hadn't suggested I speak to Steve Krug, author of *Don't Make Me Think*, but his insights transformed my approach to the process.

3. **It gets me to yes quicker**. People are more likely to respond positively when someone they know and respect has recommended them. Shortly after I set up the podcast I approached Daniel Priestley, one of my writing heros, to invite him onto the show. Not surprisingly I didn't get a response. Several months later his business partner and friend Lucy McCarraher suggested I invite him onto the show and sent a quick personal email to him to that effect: he was booked within a week.

Over to you

Based on the network map you've created, identify at least two ways you can use the process of writing your book to

- develop your network and/or
- develop your relationships

in ways that will help your business.

---

help others to help yourself

Amy Wilkinson, author of *The Creator's Code: The Six Essential Skills of Extraordinary Entrepreneurs*, recommends being nice to people.

In her book, she distilled five years of painstaking research and 10,000 pages of interview transcripts into six elegant principles or skills. The last is this: Gift small goods.

> *'A small good is a small kindness. It's something of value for someone else. The idea of gifting it is that generosity… in the modern world makes you more productive. It used to be morally right to do this. Now our reputations are very transparent, so people will know that you're a helpful colleague, and then they want to work with you. Information comes to you. Talent comes to you. Deal flow comes to you. All these things you attract by the nature of being collaborative.'*

Amy admitted that this skill was the one that most surprised her.

> *'We have a saying in the US: "Nice guys finish last." If you're collaborative, and if you're nice, and you're helping people, then maybe you're not helping yourself as much, you're wasting time, by using so much time in helping others meet objectives. The counter-intuitive truth today is that by doing that, by helping other people, you really are becoming more efficient yourself, because we choose who we work with, and other people then want to work with you, and they*

come to you, and they want to give you information,
they want to, also, build up your ideas.'

This is more than reciprocity: it's not just giving something to someone so they'll feel like they owe you. It's about consistent, principled generosity, even if you can't see a direct benefit right now.

Guy Kawasaki has a wonderful metaphor – he sees the world as divided into eaters and bakers.

'Eaters think the world is a zero-sum game: what
someone else eats, they cannot eat. Bakers do not
believe that the world is a zero-sum game because they
can bake more and bigger pies.'

I love this. I see lots of eaters, lots of people for whom the first question is always 'What's in it for me?', who live in constant fear of others stealing their ideas or being more successful. I'm not sure it ever worked well as a philosophy for life: research has proved time and time again that being nice to other people is one of the most effective ways we have to make ourselves happier. But in the modern world, where reputations are utterly transparent, it's a lousy way to do business.

After the first 10-day Business Book Proposal Challenge in 2016 I contacted a literary agent I knew and told him about one of the proposals that I thought had strong trade potential. I cheerfully set up meetings, polished the proposal and gave feedback and encouragement, with no financial interest. The book was signed, and I'm looking forward to seeing my copy soon, but the more interesting part of this was the unexpected dual benefit:

1. The agent was impressed by my attitude and we now meet regularly to discuss likely looking proposals, which helps me delight my clients, which brings in more, better-quality clients;
2. The author was so delighted that without any prompting she covered the social web with fabulous endorsements and has so far referred five new clients.

When you're writing a book, this approach translates directly into the most important assets you need: content and ideas as you write, and support and promotion once it's published. If you consistently give of yourself and your expertise you'll find it easier to attract others willing to share themselves with you, and they will more cheerfully promote you to their tribes once it's published. Yes, you'll attract a few eaters too but that's their problem. You can always bake more pie.

Over to you

- Where are your opportunities for generosity?
- Are you known as a baker or an eater?
- If you suspect you're an eater, how could you experiment with a little baking?

create a community

'Hell is other people,' Jean-Paul Sartre famously declared. I expect he'd just got back from a committee meeting or a particularly bad office Christmas party. But if you recognize that other people are in fact the lifeblood of your business, how can you go about creating a community that will not only help you write and promote your book but also support your business growth?

When I first set up the 10-day Business Book Proposal Challenge I knew it would be an incredibly useful exercise for anyone who had an idea for a book but no clue how to take it forward. I thought it might be quite a lot of work and I hoped at least a few people would stick the course.

What I hadn't anticipated was that, in just a few short days, a group of complete strangers would become a close-knit team with just the right mix of competition and collaboration, cheering each other on, offering each other ideas, encouragement and suggestions, sharing pictures of their dinners and offering to connect each other with useful contacts. Every day I watched with amazement as this community I'd created evolved in ways I could never have imagined. It was pure magic. 'Maybe I just got lucky,' I thought. But that same magic has happened every time I've run the challenge.

As I was making the final revisions for this book, holed up in a chilly cottage in Chute Forest, I was cheered by a steady stream of encouragement from the Extraordinary Business Book Club Facebook group (meaning of course there was no way I could come back and tell them I hadn't finished).

Bryony Thomas, author of *Watertight Marketing*, had a similar experience:

> *'I'd mapped the programmes, what I hadn't appreciated is the community that would come with it... I had a line on the plan which said, "Watertight Marketing community," but I hadn't really anticipated how that would feel.'*

Bryony's community is focused on her distinctive approach to marketing, which is set out in the book. Once you've bought a copy, you're invited to register it online to access additional resources such as workbooks and to become part of the Watertight community – it puts readers directly in touch with Bryony herself as well as a supportive network of advisers and peers.

I've found the magic is most powerful when there's a clear unifying purpose. The proposal challenge is a great example of this; the white-hot energy of those 10 days and the common goal of the finished proposal quickly bonds the group together, but we humans can't sustain that intensity indefinitely. The Extraordinary Business Book Club has a gentler pace but is still focused on the same journey.

Other successful online communities focus on who the members are rather than what they're doing. Be clear about what you're asking people to rally around, make it specific and inspiring.

Here are three tips from Bryony to make communities work for you (and, just as importantly, them):

1. **Make sure people are at the same stage of the journey** so nobody feels new and clueless alone. Bryony explains: 'the key difference I've made is to

bring people through the programme as a single cohort rather than them starting whenever they want to.'

2. **Buddy them up**. As with any party, some people will be happy to march right in and get involved in a conversation but other people will hang around the edges and drift out the door if they're not introduced to someone in the first few minutes. Knowing that someone in the community has your back and that you have theirs keeps you engaged and active.

3. **Be prepared to be surprised**. Your community will take your ideas in directions you've never even considered. Bryony says: 'There are a few people where I've gone back and said, "I can't take your money because I can't see that it applies, but I'd love to see you try. Let's have a go, I'll support you through it and we'll learn together." For every business, every consultant who's taken somebody through the process, I've learned something. The methodology's strengthened through use. It's been phenomenal.'

Over to you

- Where is your community?
- How are you nurturing it?
- What value are you providing?
- What opportunities for engagement are you offering?

build your street team

As you take this revolutionary approach to writing your book – engaging your network, building a community, putting out into the world the content you're creating as it takes shape – you'll find something magical happens. In addition to the people you always knew you could rely on to be supportive (thanks, Mum), you'll find you're developing a smallish group of people who are more enthusiastic and engaged than you expected. They'll be the ones sharing your updates, commenting on the material you put out, talking to other people about what you're up to, asking how you're getting on.

These people will become your street team, taking the news of your book out into the world on your behalf. Treasure them, nurture them, allow them to become even more involved and engaged, credit them in your book.

When it comes to launch day this group will come into its own: because they're invested and engaged, you can involve them in buying (discounted) copies at launch, sharing the news on social media, posting glowing reviews on Amazon and so on. (Give them what they need to do the job: a PDF proof copy so they can post reviews quickly, a 'swipe file' of email and social media copy they can use at launch, affiliate or discount codes, etc.)

But the payoff starts way before launch, as you build on their involvement and sense of belonging to something interesting and important. You can give them behind-the-scenes glimpses of the research and writing process, ask their advice on titles and/or cover designs, do a quick Facebook live when you reach a milestone like finishing the first draft, ask questions to help you develop your ideas and so on.

You can already see that there are multiple benefits here: as well as their role spreading the word about your book, the engagement and enthusiasm of your street team will reignite your own when you get sick of your book (which you almost certainly will at some point), and they will provide invaluable feedback on what's landing for them as you write. You'll get new ideas from them too: I wrote this chapter on a writing day with a few of my own street team and over lunch they gave me three new ideas for the book and five to improve my products and services.

My street team includes members of the Extraordinary Business Book Club, my bootcamp graduates, former publishing colleagues, podcast guests and a couple of friends who have nothing whatsoever to do with business books but who can always be counted on to give an honest opinion and bracing encouragement.

Treat your street team well and they'll pay back the debt a hundredfold.

Want to make it more formal? Consider creating a **brain trust**.

Over to you

- Who do you want to be in your street team?
- How can you go about engaging them? Think about the channels you can use – a private Facebook group, a networking club, a membership site, an email list.
- How can you reward them for their commitment to helping your book succeed?

create a brain trust

(I borrowed the brilliant term 'brain trust' from Bernadette Jiwa, who in her book *Hunch* thanks 'my blog readers and the members of this book's 'brain trust'... Thanks for being the catalyst for many of these ideas and for giving me a reason to show up.'[9] David Newman, author of *Do It! Marketing*, recommends something similar, which he calls his 'smart friends strategy').

Big companies have boards of directors which provide governance, a wide range of expertise, and access to useful networks. When they work well (and they don't *always* work well), board meetings are focused, challenging, supportive and collaborative.

Creating a board of directors for your book is a bit over the top but you too need focus, challenge, support and collaboration – as well as access to useful networks. The members of your street team largely select themselves but sometimes you need a smaller, more focused group. So how do you go about creating a brain trust of your own?

First, it needs planning. Just as with a board of directors, you need a balance of experience, expertise and points of view – not a homogenous group who see things just as you do and will rubber-stamp your ideas rather than offering new ones. Don't just rely on people volunteering: invite those you think will bring something of value, ask for recommendations, approach those you respect in different fields with a point of connection. Bring in visual and verbal thinkers, left- and right-brainers, introverts and extroverts.

---

[9] Jiwa, Bernadette *Hunch: Turn Your Everyday Insights Into the Next Big Thing* (Portfolio Penguin, 2017)

Second, create a way of working together: meet in person if you can, but if not, a Facebook group or Slack team can work well.

And finally, be clear what you expect of people: do you want to bounce ideas around with them, use them as a focus group for a particular part of your thinking, or get feedback on chapters as you write them? Or a combination of all of these? As part of this, be clear what's in it for them: if it's a small group you might want to name each person in the acknowledgements and give them a copy of the book; for a larger group giving more ad hoc feedback perhaps a discount code or you could offer to reciprocate in some way.

And if your brain trust works well, consider making it part of your business, not just your book: all the benefits of a board of directors without the tedious bits.

Over to you

- If your book were a business who would you want on your board?

contact hard-to-find people

As you reach upwards and outwards beyond your existing network, at some point you'll run into the problem of how to contact someone whose email address isn't easily available.

Sometimes you can overcome this with a little lateral thinking: I've tracked down direct email addresses in university staff directories, on presentations in SlideShare, in forum posts and on documents uploaded to their own or others' sites, for example.

If the person works with a large company you can often guess their email address if you can find someone else's in the same company and apply the same structural logic (e.g. firstinitial.lastname@companyname.com).

And don't forget the best route of all: who do you know who can connect you, or at least connect you to someone else who can connect you? An email from a mutual acquaintance is much harder to ignore than a cold approach, after all.

But if you've tried and failed to find an email address, how can you reach out to someone – to ask for an interview for your book, for example?

Here are a few tips:

1. Build a relationship with them on their social media platform of choice (Twitter is particularly useful for this). Don't just jump in and tweet your request at them: take time to get to know what they're saying and what they value, retweet things of particular interest to you, reply if they ask a question you can answer helpfully. You're much more likely to get a positive response if you put the groundwork in first.

Once you're in dialogue you can ask permission to email.

2. If they have an email list get on it – again, it's a great way to find out more about what makes them tick and what they care about, and if you respond to an email they've sent you, it's a different dynamic to simply sending them an email out of the blue (and more likely to get a response).

3. Find out if you have connections in common – LinkedIn can be helpful here. If you're lucky enough to be a second-degree connection you can invite them to connect with a personal message, or you can approach your mutual contact to ask for an introduction.

4. Buy them! Depending on who they are and what they do (and what you can afford, of course), buy into their services. If you respect them so much, why not? At the very least this gives you an insight into how they do what they do and you'll probably learn a huge amount. And as a customer you have the right to ask questions.

Over to you

- Think of someone you'd like to contact as part of the research for your book but whose email address you don't have.
- Use whatever method works best to find it or other contact details.
- Plan the best way to get in touch with them and then do it!

reach the rockstars

'When you're writing a book, it's a great excuse to call anyone, even a rockstar.' – Robbie Kellman Baxter

One group of 'hard-to-find' people are the 'rockstars', the people with large, established platforms and profile, whose lustre you want to borrow for your book. They'll typically receive hundreds of requests from people just like you every week. If they said yes to every one they'd never sleep. If you want them to see your email as more interesting than the average hopeful punt, you need to engage with the most fundamental of business questions: what's in it for them?

The simplest way to do this is to think carefully about your email. I approached my idol Seth Godin to invite him as a guest onto the Extraordinary Business Book Club shortly after launch, and spent a long time getting the email right. (It takes much longer to write a good short email than a long one.) I did my homework and suggested topics I thought he'd enjoy talking about, I was clear about who I was, what I was doing and why it mattered, and I made it as easy as possible for him to say yes. Here's what he said:

'Look at the email you sent me inviting me to be on the podcast. It had no apologies, it wasn't filled with dissembling and misdirection. It was clear and cogent and generous and thoughtful and it took me 10 seconds to say, "Sure! I'd be happy to do it."'

(And he's not exaggerating: it was one of the quickest responses I've ever had.)

Seth is known for his generosity and has nothing to prove – if something interests him, he'll go for it. And this is true for many rockstars, I've discovered.

But relying on piquing their interest is a risky way to go about courting rockstars. Luckily for you, when you're writing a book you're suddenly a much more interesting player in today's content economy. These are the rules by which the new economy operates:

content + platform = attention

attention + product = revenue

If you can offer a platform that will increase a rockstar's share of attention – whether that's your book, a blog, a podcast or whatever – you'll be more interesting to them than if you simply approach them for a favour.

And the best time of all to offer someone access to your platform in return for whatever it is you want from them (e.g. an endorsement or interview) is when they're promoting something new, i.e. actively seeking attention.

I regularly look at the 'next 90 days' listing for business books on Amazon because I know that if someone has a book about to launch they'll be much more receptive to an invitation to appear on my podcast.

If you want to talk to someone in a large organization, pegging your request to a recent initiative is much more likely to get you a positive response: if they're pouring money into PR to get the word out, they'd have to have a good reason NOT to talk to you about it when the opportunity presents itself. Even if the initiative isn't central to what you want to discuss with them, once you're talking you can introduce additional questions that are more aligned with your interests.

Another route is to try to meet them in person, if they're giving a talk or book signing, for example. You may not get a chance to speak to them at length but you might (though you risk doing more harm than good if you're too pushy) and you can certainly follow up with an email reminding them that you met briefly and mentioning something that particularly impressed you – again, a more difficult email to ignore than a simple cold approach.

Whatever you do, follow up. This is hard for two reasons (for me at least): firstly I need to remember to do it – I flag emails in my inbox that need action but I'm much less likely to do that for sent items – and secondly because it seems rude. It feels like I'm pestering them.

And then I remember the marketing director I used to work with who never responded to an email first time round because 'if they really want an answer they'll ask again.'

Over to you

- Who in your field would you most love to reach in connection with your book?
- How can you create a proposition that will interest them?

deliver an experience

'We need interpersonal contact. We need things to have friction and texture. Really, memory and understanding are information plus emotion.' – Tom Chatfield

A few months back I visited a wood fair with my family and we had a great day wandering around, gawking at all the exhibits and trying out some activities. As we were about to leave we spotted an apple-pressing stall. My kids were rapt: together they turned a handle to grind the apples, pounded the rough pieces into pulp, then turned the handle of the press until the juice ran – rich, fragrant and cloudy – through a muslin strainer into a jug.

The cheerful team on the stall had by this time sold all the bottles they'd brought with them. We helped them wash out and sterilize some old milk cartons so they could keep going.

Of course we bought a cartonful. We'd have bought two or three if they'd had enough. We drank it with our roast chicken dinner that night and it was amazing.

But here's the thing: we'd walked past hundreds of bottles of home-pressed apple juice and barely noticed them, let alone considered buying them. The place was crowded with stalls selling great stuff. The other apple juice might have been delicious but it was only the apple juice we'd helped to make that we got excited about.

Bookshops are full of great books: people need a reason to buy yours. You might get lucky and find someone who's actively in the market for your apple juice, the answers that only your book can provide. They will seek you out and press money into your hand. But sadly there are very, very few of them.

Most people most of the time are just wandering the stalls and there's plenty to distract them from whatever it is you're offering. If you can give them a reason to care, if you can engage and involve them with the bigger story, even – if you're REALLY good – make them feel that your success is their success, you've given them an experience, and that's what we really value.

That's why I focus so much on the community aspect of the Extraordinary Business Book Club, running writing days, inviting people to nominate their 'best bits' for the regular podcast showcase episodes and giving them behind-the-scenes glimpses into the interviews.

It's also why workshops and webinars are such powerful sales tools. A positive experience translates into a positive relationship and positive relationships are the foundation of 21st-century businesses.

Over to you

- How can you translate the topic of your book into an experience for your community?
- Are there aspects of your book that could be presented as interactions with the reader rather than simple transmission of information?

find your foreword writer

First, what's the difference between a foreword, a preface and an introduction?

I'm not sure there are legal definitions, exactly, but here's the generally understood convention:

- A **foreword** is written by someone other than the author, usually a luminary in the field, and talks about how important this topic is and what a fabulous job the author has done of tackling it.
- A **preface** is written by the author and talks about the book itself – how it came about, how it was written, how to get the most out of it and so on.
- An **introduction** is usually written by the author but, rather than introducing the book, it introduces the topic: maybe it gives some backstory (the author's own or someone else's experience) or some statistics or maybe it just sets out what the book is going to tell you and why it matters.

So now you know what a foreword is, why might you want one?

1. **Credibility**. Because it's written by someone else, a foreword is a powerful way to establish your credibility: 'Don't take my word for how fabulous I am and how great this book is – I would say that wouldn't I – but here's XXX, whom you know and like and trust and who really rates it.'
2. **Discoverability**. It's also a great secret weapon in the discoverability war: the writer of a foreword

appears as a contributor in bibliographic data, so by enlisting a big name in your field you ensure your book appears in results for that person's name – and let's face it, if you're a first-time author, the punters are more likely to be searching for an established name than for yours.

3. **Network building**. This is an opportunity to build a relationship with the luminaries in your field, those who've inspired you and shaped your ideas. Dare to dream big – who would you most love to have visibly endorsing your book? Whose name would act as guarantee and promise to potential readers that what you're saying is worth reading?

A foreword is a great opportunity to involve your preeminent peers, even your idols, in your book project.

So how do you go about approaching someone to write a foreword for you? It really depends on how well you know them. If they're a friend, or close acquaintance, you can simply talk to them – tell them about the book you're writing, tell them you'd love to have them write a foreword and take it from there.

If it's someone you know only slightly, or if you've been to their talks or read their books but they don't know you, you'll have to do a bit more work (see **contact hard-to-find people** and **reach the rockstars** for more on this).

The best approach is a short, polite email: remind them of when you met (if you did), tell them what particularly impressed you about them, then outline your book briefly and ask if they'd be willing to consider writing a foreword, or failing that an endorsement. Don't attach the whole manuscript – just a table of contents and perhaps the introduction. If they say yes you'll need to send them the full manuscript so don't approach them until you're nearly at first full draft stage at least – but well before copy-editing, otherwise you risk delaying publication while they read the book and compose their contribution.

It's never too early to start thinking about this one. Your foreword may be one of the best opportunities you have to reach out to the top figures in your field.

Over to you

- People can only say no, right? So be bold and brave – think of the person you'd most like to be associated with your book, who would have a really interesting and useful perspective to add.
- If you're nearly at full first draft stage, find an intelligent way to approach and ask them.
- If you're still at the early stages of planning or drafting your book, think of the right person and start building your relationship and connections with them, in real life, on Twitter or through mutual acquaintances, *now*.

source stories

Allan Leighton, one of the UK's top businessmen, spent much of his early career at Mars, the chocolate manufacturer, a company that believes managers need experience of life on the factory floor. On his first day he was handed a broom and instructed to sweep up any Maltesers that fell off the conveyor belt. For several frustrating, embarrassing hours he chased Maltesers as they rolled every which way but into the dustpan. Eventually one of the old lags took pity on him. He wandered over to the sweating Leighton and gently pressed his foot down on a rogue Malteser. 'You squash them,' he explained, 'then you sweep them up.'

Nigel Wilcockson at Random House Business Books told me this story, which Allan uses in his book *On Leadership*, and I still can't think of it without laughing. It's a lesson to leaders that the people who actually do the job know the job but for me it's also a reminder, when I'm engaged in something that feels frustratingly akin to chasing Maltesers, to stop and ask myself: am I missing something here?

As Nigel said, 'I defy anyone once they've heard that story to forget it.'

If you want your reader to understand an important point, you could make it earnestly with supporting facts. Or you could tell them a story that illustrates the point. The story is infinitely more likely to be absorbed and remembered.

There's chemistry behind this. Business neuroscientist Dr Lynda Shaw explains:

'When we tell a story we change it slightly according to our audience. That means that subconsciously our audience is a part of that creative process. Once they're part of that creative process, they feel more empathy for us. We start to stimulate a neurochemical called oxytocin, which is all about bonding and trusting. You have this delicious dance between the storyteller and the listener. It doesn't have to be a grand, elaborate story. It could be something that is incredibly relevant, a case study or a client that you've had or something that relates to that person. They will trust you far more, and they will feel bonded far more, and they will want to be onboard with you. It's a great persuader.'

Note that even when you're not in the room at the same time the reader still joins in the co-creation dance by visualising it for themselves and drawing out their own application, as I did with Allan Leighton's Malteser story.

Not every story has to be a full-on Hero's Journey played out step by monumental step. In fact these get old pretty quickly. The best stories are real, of course, and engaging in their own right; you don't necessarily see where they're going, then suddenly as you round the corner of the narrative – ta dah! – the point hits you between the eyes.

But what if your own life doesn't furnish all the stories you need to convey the points you want to make? Then you can go out and find them. That's what Patrick McGinnis, author of *The 10% Entrepreneur*, did:

'I interviewed dozens of people across the world, on four continents, nine countries, people in all kinds of different industries.'

How?

'The way that I found them was by putting a note on Facebook saying "Bring me the best people you can, bring me all kinds of different people." My friends really responded. Some said, "I want to be in your book," others said, "I know the perfect person for you."… Crowd-sourcing knowledge is something that is quite powerful. As a writer, it's a really great tool to bring in fresh ideas on top of your own.'

And as a bonus, the more people whose stories you include, the more people there are out there waiting for the book to be published and ready to tell all their friends about it.

Over to you

- What are the stories from your own experience that stick with you, that you find yourself telling repeatedly, that have made you who you are, that reveal how you think and why you do what you do? It can help to draw out a rough timeline of your life, identifying the 'chapters' and milestones (early school, big school, first relationship, summer job, university, first job, the time you went backpacking in Thailand, getting married, moving house, having kids, becoming a manager, quitting your job…) as a prompt. What are your most vivid memories, and why? What did these life experiences teach you? (See also **find your meaning and fascination**.)

- How can you go about sourcing stories from others? Which three or four contacts will be most useful in providing stories themselves and connecting you with others you can talk to?

set up interviews

One of the best ways to **source stories** is to set up interviews. (The BEST best way is going down the pub together but sadly that's not always possible.)

To me this has always seemed like a fairly straightforward process: identify the person you want to talk to, email them to ask if they'd be willing to speak to you, fix a time for a Skype call. And if it seems that simple to you too, move along now.

But I've come to realize that for many people – particularly but not exclusively introverts – this is anything but straightforward.

First there's the fear: what if they say no? Or ignore you? Well, at the risk of stating the blindingly obvious, in that case you're no worse off, are you? The only way you can guarantee that you WON'T get an interview is by failing to ask for one. And the first time someone says no or fails to respond you will learn an invaluable life lesson: nobody dies as a result.

Then there's the mechanics. What's the best way to approach someone to maximize your chances of a 'yes'? The general principles I set out in **reach the rockstars** hold for anyone, of course, but here's some more ideas to consider.

Setting up the interview

Subject line: make sure your email subject line is clear and includes the topic you want to talk to them about, e.g. 'Thoughts on purpose-led leadership: request for interview'. Only those absolutely ideologically opposed to the granting of interviews and with no curiosity would delete that, and if that's the case you may as well lose them immediately.

Find a connection: If you've met them before, great: use the 'You may remember me from…' line. If you're a friend of a friend, use that for all it's worth: 'Jo Bloggs suggested that I contact you…' If you've been to an event where they spoke or you've read one of their recent articles, pick up on something they said. We're all busy but we're less likely to reject out of hand something that's connected to our existing relationships and activities. And at the crudest level, the implicit flattery will make them more disposed to say yes.

Say who you are and what you want: 'I'm writing a book on…' is a powerful hook. As Robbie Kellman Baxter put it, 'It's fun to be part of a book, and you seem more serious and more interesting if you've committed to creating new intellectual property for the world. People are more interested in being part of that, so it is really worthwhile to ask.'

Be clear about what's involved: 'If you're willing, it will be an interview by Skype for no longer than 30 minutes – would any time next Wednesday or Thursday work for you?' One of the killers can be the ping-pong over dates and times: if they can't make a date and time that suits you, do whatever you have to do to fit in with them. I regularly do calls at 10pm or even 11pm in the evening and I've even arranged childcare to take calls in the holidays: this person is doing me a favour and I'm going to do everything I can to make it easy for them.

Follow up and confirm: Once it's agreed, make sure you send an immediate note to thank them and confirm the details. A day or so before the call send a reminder ('I'm very much looking forward to speaking to you on…'). This conversation isn't as important to them as it is to you so you need to take the initiative to make sure it stays front of mind. Once the interview's over, again, follow up with thanks. And once you've written the first draft, send them the section(s) containing the material from their interview as a courtesy.

Conducting the interview

It's useful to have a set of questions and some interviewees will ask you to send these through in advance. But don't follow them slavishly: if the interview moves off in a different, interesting direction, let it and ask questions that follow naturally from what's been said rather than forcing the conversation back 'on track'. You'll never discover what you don't know you don't know if you stick to the script.

I find it useful to have a few questions that I ask all interviewees as points of comparison but I also develop 'springboard' questions for each person, specific to their expertise, and these require thoughtful preparation. There are questions that only you will ask them, because they represent the intersection between your perspective and theirs, and it's a delight to be interviewed by someone who's put some thought into asking original and insightful questions. The more thought you put into the questions up front, the more engaged your interviewee is likely to be and the better the quality of the conversation.

Don't rely on taking notes – you can't listen to the answer, consider how it moves the conversation on and write it all down at the same time. Find a way of recording the conversation – I use Call Recorder with Skype. You might also want to transcribe it afterwards so that you can review it more easily and take quotes from it directly: Rev.com offers fast, accurate transcription for $1 per minute. (NB do trim down the audio file first: you don't want to be paying for them to transcribe pleasantries and technical faffing.) Always make it clear to the interviewee that you're recording, and why, and get their permission.

Using the material

Generally you can use material from an interview, including direct quotes, without a formal signed release form as long as it's clear from the start that you're conducting the interview for dissemination and possible publication and as long as they didn't specifically tell you they intended to restrict your use of the material. (Which is one reason it's worth writing a clear initial email and keeping a trail of responses.) However it's courteous to check that they're happy with how you've portrayed them so I recommend sending them the section that involves them when you're at draft stage just for information. (And if you've misunderstood something much better to find out beforehand than with a lawyer's letter after publication.)

If you've conducted an interview in a different context without the expectation that it might be made public, or if you're including material that's potentially sensitive or confidential, it's prudent to ask the interviewee to sign a release form. There are lots of free templates available on the internet (use at your own risk) but even something as simple as a signature underneath a statement like 'I consent to the use of my statements in [title of book]' would afford some legal protection.

Over to you

- Think about how you might use interviews – who do you want to speak to? What would you ask them? How could you use that material in your book (and more broadly in your business)?
- Create your interview process: an approach email template, a way of setting up and confirming times, tools for conducting/recording/transcribing the interview, and a follow-up process.
- Just do it. Start with a friendly interviewee to build your confidence, focus on them not you, and show up with curiosity and the expectation that you will both enjoy the discussion.

get feedback on your TOC

The Full Monty is one of my all-time favourite films. I love that triumphant freeze-frame finish, as the hats that were preserving the last shreds of modesty are flung aside and six blokes stand there butt-naked while the room goes wild. Nowhere to hide, nothing left to the imagination. (Except of course the camera is coyly positioned behind them.)

When I interviewed Guy Kawasaki, author of *The Art of the Start*, *The Art of Social Media* and many more books, I was inspired and terrified in roughly equal measure by his approach to building the book in public, putting up first the table of contents and then the full first draft, and inviting comments and feedback from anyone who wants to give it. This has become known in my community, inevitably I suppose, as 'doing The Full Guy Kawasaki'.

It's a way of going about things that makes complete sense to me: openness, visibility, collaboration, connection – these are all the hallmarks of the way I work, and the values underlying my business.

And for research purposes, and because I've learned that the things that scare me most are infallibly the things I most need to be doing, I did exactly that with this book. When I pressed 'post' on the blog inviting people to look at and comment on the full table of contents for this book I realized how Robert Carlyle and his mates must have felt as their hats flew across the room.

Here's what I wrote:

'If you'd like to take a look at the table of contents for This Book Means Business *here's the link: I'd love your thoughts on what sounds useful, what's missing,*

what's unclear, what's most intriguing, whether the sections and structure make sense to you, examples I should consider to illustrate the points, and pretty much any other observation you'd care to make, to be honest.'

Within a day I had some superb feedback which helped me clarify the relationship between the elements and showed me that I needed to rethink the section titles. Within a week I had a new model for the underlying structure and 10 new topics for inclusion. And just as importantly, I discovered a new level of personal accountability and commitment to the book – it was no longer safely hidden on my laptop but out in the world, being part of the conversation. I'd started to build my **street team** of fabulous engaged supporters who would go on to help me finish and launch the thing. And they weren't necessarily the people I'd expected.

Over to you

- How does the idea of sharing your table of contents make you feel?
- What are the risks?
- What are the potential benefits?
- How might you go about sharing it?

bring in the beta readers

What are beta readers? They're not professional copy-editors – this comes later. They're not your mates either, or at least not necessarily. Ideally, they're your **target reader**s but ones who know a bit about writing.

It's tempting to invite only friendly, unthreatening types to act as beta readers. Your manuscript is precious and your ego may be fragile. But sadly that's unlikely to give you much benefit. Scott Pack, author and Associate Editor at Unbound, put it this way:

> 'People that love you want you to feel good, so when you say will you look at my book, they're not going to say it's awful. They may give you some constructive criticism. I've always said if you're in a book group, who's the most critical person in that book group, who hates every book that you read? That's the sort of person that should be reading your manuscript and helping you out with it… From this point on, you are constantly going to have people telling you what they think of your project. If you're a successful author, it will be Amazon reviews and newspaper reviews, and loads of people won't like it. Get as much feedback as you can from people that you trust before you take it to the next level.'

That might sound scary but remember you're building up to putting your book out in front of the entire world, and their twitchy Amazon-reviewing fingers, so it makes all kinds of sense to get the critical feedback at this stage, while there's still time to fix it.

When I'm planning a schedule I suggest authors build in at least two weeks for themselves to review the finished manuscript and then eight weeks for beta readers: four weeks for the readers to look over the material and submit their feedback, and four weeks for the author to consider it and make the necessary changes. Often it's less formal than this: authors send a chapter on to someone with a particular interest in that topic so it can be reviewed while they work on something else. There are no hard and fast rules.

One of my authors gets her beta readers together for a quarterly 'focus group' session and finds the dynamics of the group discussion really helpful, but that can be difficult logistically.

Whoever you're using and however you're doing it, be specific about what you want back from them: if you just hand over a file and ask what they think you'll usually get either an unhelpful 'Great!' or a copy-edited file with spelling/grammar mistakes 'corrected', which isn't what you want either.

Different types of readers can give you different flavours of feedback. You can ask your ideal readers, for example, to flag places where they lose the thread of the argument, or you use words they don't understand, or where they need more information, or where metaphors and stories miss the mark, or where the pace, the level or the tone of voice are 'off' for them. Peers can check you've covered all the key issues in an area appropriately, or included all the relevant thinking/models. Authors whose writing you admire can give you pointers on style, and so on.

As a rule, beta readers can help you most by telling you what's not working. If they can tell you how they think it can be fixed that's helpful, but not as helpful as knowing what's broken: they might be wrong on the solution but if it's not working for them it's not working for them, and they can't be wrong on that. If two or more readers tell you there's a problem with a particular area, something needs fixing.

Over to you

- Identify at least three groups of beta readers (hint: one of them should be your ideal reader!).
- Identify at least two people within each group who fit the criteria: willing to help, unafraid to criticize, able to stick to deadlines.
- Plan how and when to approach them.

write with the crowd

For most books, most of the time, nobody other than a hand-selected few get to see the content before it's published. A variety of editors, of course, and perhaps the **beta readers**. But for business owners wanting to maximize the impact of their book that could be missing a trick.

In **get feedback on your TOC** I explained how Guy Kawasaki puts first his table of contents and then his full first draft up online.

> *'I literally post my Word file and I turn on the comment thing and I say, "OK, insert your comments." The bottom line is: here's my manuscript, have at it.'*

What results is not only a better book but an incredibly strong network of relationships and a group of people invested in the success of the book. As he points out:

> *'A lot of people have never interacted with an author this way, never had input into a book. They go to Amazon, buy it, and their input is inputting their credit card. There are people who can fundamentally change my book, and people have.'*

For Guy, it was a logical extension of the value he saw from sending the draft to a hand-selected set of beta readers.

> *'Even before I came up with this idea, there were 10, 15, 20 people who I respected in the world who I would send my manuscript to, and I noticed that they came back with very good comments. Then I figured*

*out that, God, maybe you don't know all the intelligent
people in the world first-hand, so maybe you should
broaden your net... When you think about it, you just
have to assume that it's the law of big numbers, and
that's what I do.'*

This is a challenging concept for many authors. How
can you charge for your finished book, they say, if you're
going to plaster the world with the first draft for free?

The reality of course is that most books fail because of
lack of attention and awareness, not a lack of adequate anti-
piracy measures. In a world where attention is the scarce
commodity, not content, those who've engaged with the
manuscript and the author directly are most likely to buy
the finished book, and to rave about it to anyone who'll
listen. This is partly their book too, after all.

'I don't see anyone else doing it my way,' Guy notes. I
think he's right and it surprises me. Flush with success from
posting my table of contents, I made the full draft of this book
available to members of the Extraordinary Business Book Club
before finalizing it, and was astonished by how many people
took the time and trouble to give incredibly useful feedback.

Over to you

- How does the idea of sharing your full first
  draft make you feel?
- What are the risks?
- What are the potential benefits?
- How might you go about sharing it?

consider crowdfunding

Part of the rich landscape of possibilities opening up before writers today is the option to crowdfund their work. Platforms such as Unbound and Readership allow authors to reach potential readers even before the book is written to communicate their vision, build enthusiasm, get feedback and – crucially – get financial commitment upfront to see the thing through.

What's not to love?

If you're an author with a compelling story to tell and the time, energy and imagination needed to build relationships with readers this is pure gold. It DOES take time, energy and imagination, however: you need to come up with a range of rewards for every pocket, put together a compelling, creative case for your book and take the time to update and engage regularly with your supporters. So is crowdfunding a good use of your precious time?

Brant Cooper believes so. He and co-author Patrick Vlaskovits crowdfunded *The Lean Entrepreneur* even though the production costs were covered by their publisher, Wiley.

'I really think all authors should do that... We wanted to generate pre orders and we wanted to have a little 'war fund', if you will, to help market during the launch and a crowdfunding campaign is a great way to do that. It's a great way to test that you've got the right messaging and that you've got those early evangelists that will be on board when you launch.'

One of my own authors, Ebonie Allard, successfully crowdfunded her book *Misfit to Maven*. As she put it:

'I want to tell my story to inspire and empower people who may feel overwhelmed or isolated or be going through any of what I went through. I want to engage with people and help them to know that there is a place where all parts of them belong, and what better way than to show my vulnerability and trust in my story and my audience than crowdfunding?...

The process of setting up the campaign was actually very simple. Coming up with rewards that will be exciting for your audience is crucial. I made a 90-second video, and created images for each reward and – ta dah!'

People support crowdfunded projects for a variety of reasons, obviously: some will do it because they like you, some will do it because a particular reward takes their fancy, most will do it because the idea catches their imagination.

Scott Pack, Associate Editor at crowdfunding publisher Unbound, puts it this way:

'It appeals to that patron-of-the-arts type idea. Everyone who supports a book at any level will get their name in the back, and they're getting their name in the back of any edition of that book that is ever published. If we sell rights to Romania and there's a Romanian edition in six years time, that book will have your name in the back... people are really happy to muck in and help make something happen.'

Both Scott and another EBBC guest David Roche, who also published through Unbound, made the point that it's often the most unexpected people who come through as your biggest supporters (like the ex-girlfriend Scott hadn't seen in years).

Is crowdfunding for you?

If you're an intensely private person, if you come over faint at the idea of asking people for money, or if you're so time-pressured that you barely have time to call your mother let alone build relationships with people off of the internet, probably not. Scott told me that on average, most people don't pledge until they've been asked three times. That takes some *cojones* on your part. But if you have those, or are prepared to grow them, it might be worth considering.

If you think this might be exactly what you've been looking for: where do you go from here?

1. Visit a few crowdfunding sites to get a feel for the projects and how they're promoted, support a few that you like the look of and see what the engagement is like from the authors and your fellow-funders.

2. If you decide to go ahead, put together a really attractive package of rewards from the tiniest (even if that's just £1) to the premium, evenly spaced so that you can appeal to all pockets. And make the premium rewards in particular really generous and compelling: Ebonie included some of her top-level programmes in the higher rewards she offered. Scott offered to edit a book for £750, well below his usual rate, and a regular publishing customer snapped up four of these. The publisher got a bargain and Scott effectively subsidized the production of his book through payment in kind.

3. Use your existing platform for all it's worth. Ebonie added her crowdfunding link to her email signature

and put a pop-up on her website, as well as regularly posting updates on Twitter and other social media channels. Mention it when you give talks, get your fans and friends and family talking about it to their networks. This is no time for reticence.

4. Deliver and be grateful. Do the best job you possibly can, meet the deadlines you promised your supporters and thank them at every opportunity. This is a social contract. Every time an author meets or exceeds the expectations of their backers, the levels of trust in the world increase that little bit, and vice versa. The trust of the crowd is even more valuable in the long term than the funding of the crowd.

Over to you

If you're considering crowdfunding, ask yourself the following questions:

- Am I willing to hustle shamelessly to make this a success?
- Do I have the time and energy to make it work?
- How will it impact me personally and professionally if I can't make it work?
- What can I provide of real value to potential backers?
- How will I use the engagement of backers to market and launch the book as well as funding its creation?

explore JVs and affiliates

Forget GSOH, the book you're writing is a much more appealing quality when it comes to attracting a potential partner. And by partner here I don't mean life partner (although, who knows...); I mean the key influencers in your field, those you'd like to get to know better.

It's a fact of life – of my life certainly and I'm pretty sure yours too – that you can't do everything on your own. Sometimes you need to bring specific skills and experience into the business by recruiting; sometimes you need to partner with another company, such as software developers, to deliver a project.

But those aren't the only options.

Entrepreneurs and small businesses are pioneering new, more flexible models for collaboration and for punching above their weight. Two of the most interesting are joint ventures and affiliate programmes, which are slightly different although the terms are often used interchangeably.

Joint ventures

Typically a joint venture is less formal than a full partnership, although it may be governed by a legal agreement. It usually involves two complementary rather than competing companies coming together to create a new product or service that will appeal to both their markets, or jointly promoting complementary products or services for mutual benefit. Because it's a two-way process, it typically involves negotiation to secure that mutual benefit. In marketing terms, however, joint ventures are more usually understood to mean an integrated marketing strategy bringing benefits to both companies. They could do reciprocal email campaigns promoting the other's product/service/event to their subscribers, for example, or share synergistic assets to create a content marketing campaign that's more than the sum of the parts.

When it's done right, a JV is a win/win: your community (and therefore you) benefit because you can offer them something of interest and value, while you leverage your partner's network and community to reach new customers. When it's done poorly, because the fit isn't right or the benefit isn't equal, it's irritating to one or both partners and their communities.

Affiliate programmes

In an affiliate relationship, there's less by way of cooperation: the provider of a product or service provides a unique affiliate link or code that another organization can use and the affiliate receives a percentage of any sales (and/or advertising revenue) derived from that link. In an affiliate relationship the product or service belongs entirely to the originating partner and the affiliate serves only to broaden its reach – there's usually little if any room for negotiation. Amazon is perhaps the most obvious example – it bills itself as the 'most popular and successful' affiliate programme on the web.

One of the best things about these models is that you don't spend a penny until the sales roll in. Here are a few ideas to get you started:

1. Enlist co-authors for mutual benefit: for example one brings the time and ability to write while the other has the profile and reach to promote the book effectively. Patrick Vlaskovits, Neil Patel and Jonas Koffler brought a complementary set of skills to the table to create *Hustle*.

2. Partner with experts in specific niches to create new 'verticals', as Michael E. Gerber did with the legendarily successful *The E-Myth Revisited* to create the E-Myth Expert series for professions as diverse as vets, financial advisers and optometrists (see **micro-niche and customize**).

3. Get the right partners on board to turbocharge your book launch: in *Launch*, Jeff Walker describes how he generated over $1m revenue in an hour from a well-planned JV product launch. And since JV partners typically direct their subscribers to sign up on your landing page you can simultaneously grow your mailing list at the same time, which in the long term is likely to be worth significantly more than the initial flurry of book sales.

4. Run a multiple JV-partner direct marketing and/or social media campaign, providing marketing copy that they can use. Make it as easy as possible for them to promote your book but allow them to adapt your copy and/or write their own too: they will have their own tone and stylistic quirks.

5. You have great content. Your potential JV partner has a great platform and network and platforms and networks run on content. Think creatively about what you can produce for them in addition to the book itself – a blog or vlog series, a webinar, free online training – to get the most effective win/win.

6. Finally, and perhaps most obviously, why not take a leaf out of Amazon's book and reward people who love your book and are willing to promote it? Offer them a bulk deal at discount to sell on to their network on a sale or return basis, or if you sell your book direct from your own site create an affiliate code that earns them a cut every time someone buys it on their recommendation.

NB Seth Godin offers a bulk discount to anyone, making the whole world a distribution engine for his books:

'One person has bought six 99-packs. Every month or two, he comes back. In a 99-pack, you get 120 copies. He's bought 120 books, month, after month, after month. Clearly, he's doing something with them, and I don't have to treat him like a bookstore. I just treat him like a peer, who has decided that for whatever commercial reason, it's in his interest to distribute hundreds and hundreds of my book.'

In a world of horizontal selling and peer recommendations this makes all kinds of sense.

Over to you

- Identify a potential JV or affiliate partner.
- Design an offer that's a win/win for both of you.
- Pitch it and see what happens.

GROWING YOURSELF

Writing a book is so much more than simply publishing a book. Joanna Penn talked to me about 'the anti-climax of publication', the realization that the moment of publication was never really what this was about.

> *'It's the writing that's the point, the transformation comes with the writing and the publication is just the start of your next journey which is book marketing, or writing the next book... The biggest change for me over the last 10 years is not that [the fear and self-doubt] have disappeared, it's that I now know they are part of the process, so I'm not afraid of them.'*

Writing your book can do more than improve your bottom line: it can stretch and shape you into the person you want to become.

Apart from fear (see **A note about fear**), there are two main reasons why business owners who want to write a book haven't yet done so: lack of time and lack of clarity.

Doing the time

Time is the one thing that no business owner has enough of. If you're successful, you've probably spent years refining your to-do list to ensure you focus only on the activities that will bring the biggest return. Which means that you'll need to be really clear about the benefit your book will bring to your business before you allow yourself to spend time on it.

In this section you'll find insights and ideas that will help you work more effectively and focus your most precious resource, your attention, on making your book work for your business.

But if you're not convinced of the usefulness of writing, and if you're not clear what you're saying and why, you won't find the time to do it, simple as that.

Getting clear

Which brings us to the second point: clarity. We're more likely to find time to do what inspires and energizes us, what we know is essential for our personal and professional growth, so getting clarity is the first step. If you're not clear on what you're trying to say, even if you conquer your fear and set aside time, you'll end up writing yourself into a hole. At which point the fear resurfaces – 'You have nothing to say! You're a fraud! Better keep quiet!' – and with a sense of guilty relief you'll let the urgent stuff crowd out the time you'd ring-fenced for writing.

But, ironically, it's writing itself that gives us the clarity to write. As Orna Ross, head of the Independent Authors Alliance (ALLi), put it, 'writing is one of the most undervalued things that we have in our armoury as people.'

That's why in this section you'll discover some thoughtful, practical ways in which you can use the writing of your book as a tool for self-development, including overcoming fear and procrastination and getting clarity.

rich reading

*NB this kind of immersive reading is important but it doesn't scale well. Keep rich reading for the most interesting books in your field and for the rest use the **rapid reading** technique.*

In computing they talk about GIGO, 'garbage in, garbage out'. When it comes to writing, where your brain does the processing rather than a CPU, it's GRIGWO: good reading in, good writing out.

So many of the authors I've spoken to on the podcast have talked about the importance of reading: reading for its own sake, reading for competitive advantage, reading as a writer, and what reading does for us in an increasingly digital world.

What's that, you say? Reading for competitive advantage? Well, yes.

Barbara Gray, author of *Ubernomics*, features on her company's site BradyCap a 'library' of books she describes as 'the foundation of our intellectual asset base'. She also credits a whole stack of other books as resources at the back of her own.

As you'd expect from an asset manager, she gives the idea of reading as preparation for writing a financial spin:

> *'[Authors] build their ideas upon other people's ideas. If you look at the footnotes/endnotes of most business strategy books they've referenced so many people… from the perspective of an analyst that's called Mosaic Theory: taking unrelated pieces of information, putting them together, and coming up with a thesis that will give you insight into whether to buy or sell stock.'*

We only make good decisions when we have good information, which makes reading good books not just a pleasure but a business obligation. You're not 'just reading', you're making one of the smartest investments ever.

What should you read? There are three broad categories:

1. **In your field**

   Whatever you're writing about and whether you like it or not, there are already books out there by good authors on that subject. And that's a *good* thing: it shows there's an appetite out there. Books aren't like fridges, get one and you're good for the next 10 years – people buy multiple books on subjects they care about. But you need to know the lie of the land: what are the hot topics, the models and methodologies your competitors are using, the emerging ideas and vocabularies. Don't stop at books: immerse yourself in blogs, podcasts, journal articles and any other quality content that's leading the conversation in your area, in preparation for adding your own contribution.

2. **In adjacent fields**

   Maria Popova, blogger at BrainPickings, who tellingly describes herself as 'a reader who writes', defines creativity as 'the ability to connect the seemingly unconnected and meld existing knowledge into new insight about some element of how the world works.'[10] Emma Serlin fused her experience as an actor and director with her studies in psychology to create The Serlin Method™ for

---

[10] www.copyblogger.com/how-maria-popova-writes/

communicating more effectively. Eric Ries took agile software development and married it to Steve Blank's theories on entrepreneurship to create *The Lean Startup*. What's going on in the field just over the fence from you, or even a few fields along, and what new light could that shed on your topic?

3. **Just generally out there**

There are enough business books out there to keep you reading for centuries but that's not a balanced diet. Make space for stuff that, on the surface at least, has no obvious connection to what you're writing but which appeals to you. Read fiction, comedy, autobiography – whatever you like as long as the writing is good – and you'll find the narrative devices, the timing of the jokes, the rhythm and shape of the storytelling start to inform your own writing. You'll also be a lot more fun at dinner parties.

But if you're planning to get involved in the conversation as an author consider taking reading one step further. It doesn't have to be a passive, one-way activity.

As Seth Godin put it:

> '*It's so easy to imagine that people are doing things to us – that they are organizing this event to us, they are writing this book to us, they are writing this blog to us, but it's not true. They're doing it with us. You have an obligation… If you read a book and it works, give the book to someone else. Spread the word. This is the obligation of the audience… good audiences make good performances.*'

What kind of a reader are you? Do you put your back into it? Do you step up to your obligation as part of the unspoken deal with the writer to enable them to give of their best or is half your attention on your phone? When you read something good, read it properly. Bring all your insight and experience to it and use it to create something in your turn. You could even reach out to the writer and let them know what worked for you, what ideas it triggered in your head, what results you had, how much you appreciated their expertise and the time and trouble they took to communicate it to you.

Not only will you get more from the book because you'll have made yourself consider what it's really meant to you, you'll get more from it as a writer because you'll have looked under the hood to better understand how the author did it. And you may even establish a relationship with that author which will build your professional network and perhaps even benefit your book.

Over to you

- Which book in your area have you read recently that's most inspired you? (If you haven't go and find a likely looking candidate and read it thoughtfully!)
- How can you move the conversation that the author started on to the next stage and add your own ideas: for example by sharing the book with a contact who'll find it useful and explaining why, blogging about it, or contacting the author directly?

rapid reading

When I started the Extraordinary Business Book Club, I naïvely assumed I'd read every book ahead of every interview using that rich reading technique. I very quickly realized I'd get little else done in the week. So I developed a way of reading a book rapidly: absorbing the key points and understanding its flow without reading every word.

This technique allows you to listen in on the conversation in and around your field without dedicating your life to the job, and is a great way of researching for the writing of your book too.

It owes a lot to Peter Bregman's article in *Harvard Business Review*, 'How to Read a Book a Week'[11] – or more accurately to Bregman's college professor Michael Jimenez, who taught him the difference between reading and understanding a non-fiction book.

Bregman recommends starting with the author: first read their biography to get a sense of their background and experience to help you put their book into perspective.

Publishers like me put a lot of time and energy into helping readers like you. We use titles that communicate what the book's about and who it's for, we create back cover copy and marketing blurbs that set out the key ideas, and highlight what's different and distinctive about this author and this approach. So don't simply dive into the book on page 1 – start with these useful summaries of the key ideas.

The table of contents is another vital tool for readers: it's the map of the book and you can use it not only to grasp

---

[11] https://hbr.org/2016/02/how-to-read-a-book-a-week

the book's scope and shape but to zoom in on the areas of particular interest to you.

It's useful too to read reviews, particularly mid-ranking reviews, which tend to be more thoughtful and nuanced. What did people find particularly helpful and where do they feel the book falls down?

(NB so far you don't even have to have bought the book: all this information is freely available on Amazon on the book's sales page and through the 'look inside' function.)

This will probably be enough for you to get a sense of whether it's worth taking your reading any further. If you decide to go ahead and buy the book, Bregman suggests you read the introduction, in which the author sets out the problem they're addressing and their approach to it, and the conclusion, which summarizes their argument, and then skim the first and last paragraph of each chapter to see how it advances the argument – if it's particularly interesting/ relevant you can switch to rich reading, of course.

Over to you

- Which book has been sitting on your 'to-read' list for months?
- Set aside half an hour to do a 'rapid read' of the freely available material.
- Identify at least one key interesting insight or idea from it.
- Decide whether it's worth going on to **rich reading**.

turn your reading into a conversation

Both **rich reading** and **rapid reading** are useful but, if you want to take it to another level, write notes as you read to turn the passive act of reading into a dialogue with the author. In a sense it doesn't really matter *how* you do it: the mere act of taking notes forces you to engage actively with the text and that means you'll understand what you're reading and retain it more effectively.

There's more in the writing section about how to take notes and organize your research but this tip is focused on taking notes as a way of understanding more deeply and developing your own thinking.

The way I do this is simply to take a fresh sheet of A4 paper and put the title of the book and the author's name at the top. Then I draw a line down the middle of the page, like this:

Title of Book by A. N. Author	

Then, whether I'm reading richly or rapidly, I simply notice what I notice and jot it down on the left-hand side. So far so standard note-taking procedure. But what takes it to the next level is what happens in the right-hand column, which I call my 'So What?' column. What does that tip/fact/observation/insight mean for me and my business? What possibility or action does it suggest? How might it apply in other, more relevant areas?

I imagine it as a personal coaching session with the author, as if they were sitting with me bringing their wisdom to help me thrash through the issues I'm facing. Sometimes it's a 'yes, but…' comment; more usually it's 'yes, and…' or 'ooh, that gives me an idea…'

Here's an example from one of the first books I ever read (or rather, re-read) using this system, Michael E. Gerber's *The E-Myth Revisited*, which fed directly into a product I was creating at the time:

The E-Myth Revisited by Michael E. Gerber	
'Go to work ON your business rather than IN it.' - most people spend most time working IN the business, not acting as CEO but as technician.	Useful for bootcamp structure? Consider breaking into two strands: ON the book (ie building business, marketing etc) and IN the book (ie structure, writing etc).

You'll find that in many cases the results of this engaged, conversational thinking will feed into your book and other content such as blogs, which opens out the conversation even more.

For me, this is the most satisfying way of all to read: not simply consuming but co-creating new insights and ideas along with the author. It's also a great technique for note taking at conferences and events: don't just jot down what the speaker's saying, add a column for the 'aha' insights you come up with yourself.

Over to you

- Identify a book that you know will be of interest and worth rich reading.
- Try this technique or a similar way of bringing your own perspective into your notes and see what emerges.

writing as a tool for reflection

From reading, as naturally as night follows day, to writing.

'Most of the people I know who are good at writing are good at thinking. I'm going to argue that the writing makes you a better thinker not just that good thinkers become writers.' – Seth Godin

'You become more... observant. You think, "Well, that's interesting. Why is that interesting? I might write about that. What do I think about that? What do I want to say about that?"' – Euan Semple[12]

'It seems to me that what writing does for me is two things. It forces me to give form to the formless. I could just bliss out a lot. I could just hang out and connect and listen to people and be a space in which they get more creative and perform better and do better in their lives. Writing... makes me put words to the music. Then you've got a song.' – Michael Neill

If you won't take my word for it, listen to them.

Writing is an important practice for business leaders and entrepreneurs. It has an intrinsic value way beyond all the practical business benefits of establishing expert authority, increasing discoverability and building trust.

---

[12] In conversation, October 2015.

What happens when you write?

The fact is that writing changes us. It takes us below the surface of the superficial thinking and communicating we do every day to something deeper and more valuable. It helps us, it forces us to notice thoughts and beliefs and connections and intuitions we didn't know were there until they appear on the page in front of us when we're in flow and we read back and say, 'Aha! Of course!' and occasionally, 'Who wrote this? This is brilliant.' And once you've seen, you can't unsee. You take that new understanding and clarity back into the world of action and busyness and you think and behave differently because of it.

A similar thing can happen when you're speaking; the insights can appear and surprise you. But when you speak it happens in real time. You can't slow the pace if you need to and the thread of the thought is gone almost as it appears (unless you record it). When you speak, unless it's to the dog, you don't usually own the thinking space in the way that you do when you write. That can be a good thing: sometimes the other person or people are the flint you need to strike your spark.

But for sustained thinking and for exploring an insight, one of those elusive seen-out-of-the-corner-of-your-eye insights, the noise and speed of conversation are no good. They scare them away. Writing gives space and quiet for the shyest, deepest, most original parts of us to emerge into the daylight, without the fear of being prematurely judged. How do we know if an idea has any value, any truth until we've articulated it? We need space to find out what it is we think before we risk putting it in front of someone and saying, 'Is it any good?'

Think like a writer and everything becomes grist to the mill. A bad day becomes a good story. Developing a writing habit forces us to reflect on what happens, on our own decisions and actions and those of others. And as Socrates pointed out, 'The unexamined life is not worth living.'

Your book is your writing habit writ large. One of the unexpected gifts it will give you is more clarity in your business strategy, a deeper understanding of your message and your place in the world, and the way you put that across in every aspect of your communication.

Someone working through the 10-day Business Book Proposal Challenge recently posted: 'For the first time ever I can clearly say what I do for a living and who I AM.'

And don't think this is just a tool for beginners. I asked Michael Neill whether writing his books had changed him and this was his response:

'Oh it always does: it's one of the reasons to write, as far as I'm concerned.... I'd been teaching this stuff for 7 years when I wrote the book so it wasn't new to me, but I knew that writing it would force me to a new level of clarity.'

Over to you

- Think of an experience this week – good or bad, it doesn't matter. It'll soon be forgotten but it's got something to teach you.
- Take just 15 minutes to write about it:
  - What happened, and why?
  - How did it affect you?
  - What would you do differently next time?
  - What does it teach you about yourself?
  - What else can you learn from it?

freewriting

Mark Levy, author of the brilliant *Accidental Genius*, first introduced me to the idea of freewriting but he got it from Peter Elbow's *Writing with Power* (1998). That's ideas for you; they take on their own life once you put them out in a book.

The basic idea is to uncouple the act of writing from the idea of being read, to use it instead (as Levy puts it) as 'a spigot to the deepest part of the mind'. The thinking unspools loosely, even chaotically, from your brain through the pen to paper (or, if you prefer and if you're a REALLY fast typist, through the keyboard to the screen), and as it does so it forces you to follow the thread wherever it takes you, without judgement, creating new connections and insights along the way.

It's more powerful than simply sitting and thinking because the thread of your thought remains unbroken, and because – unlike thought – writing leaves a trail, so you can go back and pick out the golden moments of clarity from the muddle.

Orna Ross, head of the Alliance of Independent Authors ALLi, uses the mnemonic FREE when she's teaching freewriting: Fast, Raw, Exact, Easy.

'The most important thing there is fast. When I teach it in a workshop situation, I will say, "Go," and they all write as fast as they possibly can until I say "Stop," and raw means that when you're writing like that, you don't pay any attention to what your English teacher taught you about grammar, punctuation, spelling, any of that. You just keep on writing as fast as you can, and

raw too, in the sense that when you write that fast, sometimes you'll find you're writing something you'd rather not write. So it's about revealing that thought beneath the thought that you might not be aware of.

Exact is about using the specific detail of your own life, and taking a second or two to write the extra words that really describe something, so rather than saying, say, "A fruit bowl," you would say, "Green grapes," or, "Green grapes going off," or something that would just give the essential detail, but easy accompanies fast, so it's a flow kind of thing.

And Easy – it's a very natural process, except we've been taught to think, and second thoughts, and third thoughts.'

Robbie Kellman Baxter also discovered the power of writing as a thinking tool as she wrote *The Membership Economy*:

'When I have a problem and I don't know the answer. I'll open a clean document… and I'll say, "I want to be able to answer this question but I don't know how, and the reason I don't know how is because…", and then I just go from there, and usually I come up with a much better way of framing the problem and sometimes an actual answer.'

The other great benefit of freewriting, quite apart from its use as a thinking tool, is that it primes the pump for writing your book. It gets you into the habit of writing often and openly and helps you manage the fear of committing words to paper that paralyzes many authors. Once you know that you can write usefully for yourself, you always have a place to start. And once you know that you can write yourself out of any hole, indeed that writing is perhaps the best route out of a hole, you'll never be stumped by writer's block.

Over to you

- Take an aspect of your business that isn't quite clear, for example:
  - Your target market
  - What it is that makes you distinctive
  - How an idea you've just had, or something that's just happened in the world, impacts on your field.
- Set the timer for 15 minutes and just write about it (or dictate, if you prefer). Remember 'FREE': Fast, Raw, Exact, Easy. Nobody's going to see this material; it's just you and your ideas.
- What do you notice? (See also **Morning Pages**.)

Morning Pages

You know when four different people tell you how great something is in the space of a week? That was the point at which I felt compelled to investigate Morning Pages – a practice recommended by Julia Cameron in *The Artist's Way*.

Here's how it works: you write three sides of letter paper (A4 for Brits) in longhand every morning immediately upon waking. This, it seems, is your most creative state, before you buckle on your ego and busyness for the day.

I discovered very early that it takes on average until the middle of the second page before the thoughts coalesce and I shift from burble into purposeful flow.

Morning Pages works because it provides a safe space to do that. Hell, it practically forces you to do it. It's a way to create that new synaptic sequence: it gives you space and time to 'feel' the insight then forces you to articulate it. When I'm in flow, it's impossible to tell whether I'm writing down the thoughts as they come or thinking them into being as I write. As William Zinsser pointed out, 'Writing, learning and thinking are the same process.'[13]

I'm an off-the-scale extrovert, but in my (admittedly sporadic) Morning Pages ritual I uncover deep within myself a creative introvert. It has transformed my attitude to my own creativity completely and removed the terror of the blank page.

Like freewriting, it's also a fabulous way to prime the pump for writing your book and get you into the writing

---

[13] *Writing to Learn: How to Write – and Think – Clearly About Any Subject at All* (2013)

habit. It's different from freewriting in that there's no agenda: it's about accessing the deepest, most creative part of your brain, rather than using writing as a tool to help you unravel a specific knot.

But perhaps the most wonderful thing about the practice is that, as Cameron says, 'There is no wrong way to do Morning Pages.'

Over to you

- Try out a practice of Morning Pages for at least a week. Don't censor or judge your writing.
- Keep going until you've filled three sides each day.
- See what emerges and notice what you discover about yourself.

find your meaning and fascination

One of the most common pieces of advice for business book authors – and one that I often repeat myself – is to focus on the reader. What problem do they have, what is it that they're seeking, what language will resonate with them?

That's important but it's not the whole story. As automobile pioneer Henry Ford famously said, if he'd asked people what they wanted they'd have said 'faster horses'.

If you're writing a book to position yourself as a thought leader, starting out by positioning yourself as a follower, even if that's following your own potential readers, makes no sense: all you'll create is an endless cyclical echo chamber.

Writing coach and positioning expert Mark Levy put it this way:

> *'If you look to your audience first… they're just going to have you repeat what they've already considered safe. What they've pre-chewed for you. You're not going to be any thought leader by doing that.'*

His recommendation?

> *'You take all your meaning and your fascination and you put it down on paper. Then you look at what it is you're most excited about in life and then you look at your audience and say, "Where do they most need help? What could they be most excited about?" You find a place from column A and column B where they coincide and you say, "Here's the thing that I can help them with based on what's honest for me."'*

For Levy, 'meaning and fascination' means the lint that's stuck in your mental filter, the stuff that for whatever reason you can't forget, the philosophy, the ideas, the stories that fascinate you and in which you find your own meaning and significance.

Each person's meaning and fascination pile is different: yours will be a product of your unique life and work experiences, the relationships and conversations you've had, the books you've read, all processed by your unique perspective and cognition. That's where thought leadership starts, if you dare to explore and express it.

Over to you

What's in your meaning and fascination pile?

- Take at least 15 minutes of uninterrupted time and mind map around the topic of your book the ideas and stories that hold meaning and significance for you.
- Spin off the ideas into other areas – often the insight comes when you recognize parallels between different areas of your life – and you can use your understanding of one to illuminate the other in an entirely new way.

know thyself – Gretchen Rubin's Four Tendencies

One of the most fundamental questions to ask yourself when you decide to write a book is: what kind of writer are you? The more clearly you understand your strengths and preferences, the more likely you are to find a way of writing that works for you.

You might like to think for example that you're the kind of person who sets a goal and then single-mindedly does whatever's necessary to achieve it but the chances are you're not. There aren't many of those in the world (and if it makes you feel better they tend to be quite dull at parties).

Bec Evans, founder of writing productivity app Prolifiko, introduced me to Gretchen Rubin's 'Four Tendencies' framework,[14] which I've found an incredibly helpful way not only to trick myself into being more productive but also as a way of working out what makes my clients tick. Rubin divides the world into Upholders, Obligers, Questioners and Rebels.

Upholders are those who say to themselves, 'I'm going to do X,' and then they quietly go away and do it. Just the fact that they've promised themselves they will achieve something is enough to make them deliver on that promise. They're a rare breed.

If you're an Upholder good for you. You're probably too busy finishing your final edit and planning the launch party to have bought this book anyway so it's safe for me

---

[14] Rubin, Gretchen *Better Than Before: What I Learned About Making and Breaking Habits – to Sleep More, Quit Sugar, Procrastinate Less, and Generally Build a Happier Life* (Two Roads, 2016)

to say how unbelievably irritating the rest of us find you. While simultaneously wanting to be you.

Obligers are much more likely to do the thing they've promised if they've promised it to someone else, not just themselves. If you find the only way to get yourself to the gym is to promise to pick up a friend on the way, pay attention.

If you're an Obliger like me – and there are many of us – joining a writing community or making yourself publicly accountable is a good way of tricking yourself into making progress. Now you HAVE to write, right?

Questioners are the Spocks of the world: they will do something only if and when they understand why it matters. They won't spend their precious time and energy putting together a content strategy just because someone tells them it's a good idea: they want to know exactly what's involved and how it's going to benefit them before they commit. (I have a Questioner child. 'You need to get dressed now.' 'Why?')

If you're a Questioner, you'll find the strategic thinking and title selection tools in **Growing your business** particularly useful: you need to be really clear on WHY you're writing this book and what it's going to do for your business before you'll knuckle down and do the work.

Rebels only need to see an instruction or an expectation to immediately feel an irresistible urge to do the opposite. (I have a Rebel child too.)

If you're a Rebel, well, good luck. You probably shouldn't write a book.[15]

---

[15] See what I did there? Now I've told you not to, you want to, right? You're welcome. I've been practising this manoeuvre for years now.

Over to you

- Take Gretchen Rubin's tendencies quiz (www. surveygizmo.com/s3/3163256/Gretchen-Rubin-s-Quiz-The-Four-Tendencies-Fall2016).
- Once you've discovered what tendency you are, think about what that means for your writing practice.
- What do you need to do or put in place to give yourself the best chance of making your writing habit stick?

know thyself – where do you get your energy?

One of the most fundamental personality traits, common to almost every method of measurement, is the tendency towards extraversion or introversion. It's often misunderstood: introversion is not the same as shyness and extroverts don't necessarily like being the centre of attention. The distinction in psychology, following Carl Jung's definition, is more about how we energize ourselves. Jung described extroverts as characterized by 'an outward flow of energy (libido) – an interest in events, in people and things, a relationship with them, and a dependence on them.' Introversion on the other hand was, he said, characterized by 'an inward flowing of personal energy – a withdrawal concentrating on subjective factors.'[16]

The popular MBTI personality profiling takes this distinction as one of its key dimensions but it's worth bearing in mind too that extraversion and introversion are simply points on a continuum. Most of us are a blend and few of us are fixed: even someone as high on the Myers-Briggs extraversion axis as me needs quality time alone sometimes, and most introverts can pony on a stage with the best of them when necessary.

It's tempting to say we should forget the distinction and accept that we're all ambiverts, able to swing either way, energetically speaking. But for most of us Jung's point holds true: there's a default preference. If I'm feeling threatened, anxious or even ill I tend to become more introverted. 'She's not herself today,' my friends might say and they're

---

[16] *Psychological Types* (1921)

right: when I 'become myself' again, when things are back to normal and my mental state bobs back to its usual level, the extraversion kicks back in. I'm ready to reengage and reenergize myself.

Joanna Pieters, host of the Creative Life Show podcast and herself an introvert, offered an interesting analysis of what can happen to the two types under pressure, and the dangers of both:

> *'The danger for an introvert is an increased likelihood that they'll go inwards for a solution to a problem, either by just working harder or thinking more intensively. And under pressure, they'll find the outwards-facing interactions harder to get value from, and they may well be less likely to do them.*
>
> *However, for an extrovert under pressure, they're perhaps more likely to have conversations, but the danger is that they can be unfocused, because their drive is about feeling better by having enjoyable interactions. And an extrovert in that situation doesn't always take the time to evaluate or internalize what's going on. For writing or other solitary activities, a disciplined extrovert can also decide that being social is the 'wrong' thing to do, so cut it out, but miss out on those opportunities.'*[17]

---

[17] Discussion in the Extraordinary Business Book Club Facebook group, March 2017.

Over to you

- If you don't already know it, take a personality test to discover your own preference. The full Myers-Briggs test takes time and a skilled practitioner but there are several quick-and-dirty versions out there that, taken with a grain of salt, can give some interesting insights.
- Assuming you know your type, think about what that means for how you research, write and tell people about your book. What do you particularly need to look out for, exploit or avoid? There are some useful tips in the next two chapters.

know thyself – tips for extroverts

As mentioned in the previous chapter, I am undeniably an extrovert. Which is irritating. It's so much cooler being an introvert. But I just can't help myself: I love being with people. I find it physically impossible to stay silent if an interesting conversation is happening near me. (And it's not just me: my mother once spent nearly two hours on the phone to a wrong number.)

Times being an extrovert has been useful:

- running workshops
- leading training courses
- talking to random interesting people on trains
- managing a team
- coaching and facilitating teams
- fundraising
- networking
- hosting children's parties
- interviewing guests for The Extraordinary Business Book Club podcast
- coaching people how to write their book.

Times being an extrovert has been a complete disaster:

- sitting down to write my own book.

Ironic, eh?

We extroverts get our energy and ideas from bouncing off others. I'm not a hopeless case: I am perfectly capable of sitting alone and Getting Stuff Done without the TV on in the background or calling a friend every five minutes. But sitting alone day after day leaves me feeling shrivelled and diminished. I've cheerfully written books to commission – that's just Getting Stuff Done. But when I first sat down to write this book, the book that would articulate my philosophy of writing and business and books, I could feel the energy leaching out of me as I sat alone and stared at the screen.

When I need energy and ideas and inspiration, I get them through connection. I discover what I think and what needs to be done next by talking it through with one of my wonderful, long-suffering entrepreneur buddies. An idea will materialize in that magical inter-person space so that neither of us can say who first thought it: we brought it into being together like metaphysical parents.

It's no coincidence that the vast majority of writers are introverts, or at least ambiverts. But you *can* write a book as a full-on extrovert; you just need to balance the actual sitting and writing with opportunities to access the energy you need.

Here are some suggestions based on what worked for me:

1. Take part in **accountability challenges**. Bec Evans at Prolifiko got me out of the starting blocks with a simple but effective 5-day challenge, and I run a regular 10-day Business Book Proposal Challenge that does the same for others.
2. Try **talking**. Even alone in a room – get up and walk around and talk out loud to find out what it is you're trying to say. I have two clients who are dictating rather than writing their books because that's how

they think best. This has the added advantage of keeping the tone direct and conversational. If you have a picture of your ideal reader pinned on the wall, and you're talking directly to him or her, so much the better.

3. **Write with others**. Ideally physically sitting and writing together. Big chunks of this book were written on writing days with other members of the Extraordinary Business Book Club as we all sat in a room ignoring each other until the coffee break. I finished the first draft house-sitting in Devon with a friend who was also trying to finish her book, taking breaks to eat and run together. When I can't meet up with fellow writers, I head to a library or coffee shop. But even when I can't get out (say I'm writing early in the morning while the kids are asleep), just knowing someone else is sitting down in their house to write at the same time as me and checking in with them by email at the start and finish is a huge help.

4. Keep part of your brain as an open tab for your book and **notice all the ideas and insights** that come to you as you interact with others in the normal course of life. Capture them in whatever way works best for you – Evernote is great for this. I regularly send myself voice memos immediately after an interesting conversation. Build up a store of hot coals to ignite your next solo thinking and writing session rather than having to create from cold each time.

5. **Make your extraversion work for you**. Interview people, invite them to contribute, curate as well

as creating. I wrote this book in public, getting tips and feedback from authors and experts and reporting back on my progress week by week on the Extraordinary Business Book Club podcast. I know introvert friends who would rather die than contemplate this but I also know that it worked brilliantly for me. Charles Dickens knew all about this – he fuelled his writing with talks, travel, serialization, amateur dramatics, long walks with fellow authors, correspondence with fans. Find out what works for you and do it, no matter how crazy it seems to someone else.

6. Extrovert writers have **tools** available to them today Dickens could only have dreamed of. Join the Extraordinary Business Book Club Facebook group or another online writing community, take part in NaNonFiWriMo, sign up to social productivity tools like Prolifiko, report on your progress via Twitter, Facebook live from your writing den – find what works for you.

7. Finally, even an off-the-scale extrovert like me has a tiny introvert buried deep within. **Make friends with that introvert**. Find out how to get it on your side. Mine likes to go running – there's something about the oxygen, endorphins, the stimulation of being outdoors, together with the mindless rhythm of the legs, that empowers my introvert and enables it/me to reflect and create from the inside out. I actually prefer running alone and without music now that I've discovered this. The practice of **Morning Pages** has also been a revelation, a safe

place to look inwards and find unexpected insights and clarity.

The great news for extroverts of course is that if they can get over the hurdle of actually writing the book, their propensity for talking to strangers really comes into its own in the second, equally important and equally creative stage of bringing a book into the world: promotion.

Publishing a book today involves promoting the pants off it on social media, as a speaker, to anyone who'll listen. Hang on to that as you struggle through the writing phase. Your time will come.

Over to you

- If you're an extrovert, how can you use that to your advantage as you write your book?
- How can you overcome the disadvantages?

know thyself – tips for introverts

As an extrovert, I didn't feel qualified to write this article so I drafted in some friends to help by posting a plea in the Extraordinary Business Book Club group.

Bec Evans described the process of writing as an introvert so beautifully that I immediately wanted a personality transplant.

> 'I absolutely love sitting at my desk, alone in the quiet to write. I love being inside my head with the ideas and watching them take shape, first of all within me, then on to the page. I do like talking to people about stuff, and believe that collaboration helps, but I have to have a sense of the idea first. I hate noise, interruption, distraction.'

Many introverts find the kind of exuberant chatting that energizes me exhausting. As blogging guru Sarah Arrow put it: 'If I'd wanted to talk to people I wouldn't have started writing.'

Whereas extroverts can use conversations to catalyse and expand their ideas by thinking out loud and bouncing off others' energy, introverts may prefer to use them to generate interesting input, which they can then take and process quietly alone when the conditions for writing and thinking are better suited to their style.

Some felt that chatting is especially uncomfortable when they themselves are under the spotlight. Grace Marshall, author of *How to be Really Productive*, has learned a trick to regain control: 'I turn it around on them. "So, tell me about you? What are you working on?"'

If you're an introvert, however, writing itself is likely to be the easy bit. The difficulties come when you look beyond the satisfying, deep work of writing to the challenges of building an author platform and promoting your book. Make it easier on yourself by using the process of writing to connect with others online, thoughtfully and selectively, in a way that chimes with who you are and how you are, and quietly build a network of people who are aware of and engaged with your book (see **Growing your platform** for more on this).

Over to you

- If you're an introvert, how can you use that to your advantage as you write your book?
- How can you overcome the disadvantages?

Part 2

WRITING YOUR BOOK

In Part 2 we're going to look at the mechanics of writing. However expert you may be in your field, there's no reason why you should be an expert writer but these tips from successful business book authors will help you write a better book, faster, and enjoy it more.

This part of the book starts with getting clear on what you're writing, as that's the groundwork for everything else, and then addresses the mechanics of making it happen, including some advanced ninja tips from successful writers. Finally there are some ideas to take you beyond the book, putting it in its bigger business context.

As you've already discovered, writing is a tool for both personal and business development so lean into the process and enjoy the journey.

Once you've mastered writing as a personal and professional skill you won't stop when you finish your book: think of this as a new regular discipline, like exercise or meditation, and work out whatever way of doing it suits you best.

GETTING CLEAR

Before you create book.doc and start typing, it's worth spending some time thinking about what exactly you're going to say, and how it's going to be put together.

In this section we'll explore how you go about capturing lightning in a bottle. It's not magic, it just feels that way.

draw out your book

I realize kicking off a section on writing by talking about drawing seems bonkers but as a business author you're dealing in ideas, and the first step in communicating those ideas is to understand them fully yourself – which is often harder than it sounds.

Writing is a great thinking tool but drawing can be an even more fundamental way to get clear on what it is you're actually saying. My last boss, one of the most intelligent men I have ever met, once told me, 'I got to the age of 50 before I realized that if I drew a problem I could solve it in half the time.'

Visualising your ideas has a double benefit: for you as author – to help you get clear on what it is you're saying and how your ideas fit together and flow – but also for the reader.

Heather McGowan, academic entrepreneur and futurist, uses this cognitive trick extensively, beginning with the initial idea:

> 'I don't usually start writing anything. I start drawing a lot of things. My starting process is: how would I put this on a single page so that people can understand it with very few words using shapes and different types of frameworks? I usually start with a series of frameworks that tell the story to me in my head and then after that I write.'

I drew out this book before I began writing it and the structure and progression evolved out of that early scruffy drawing:

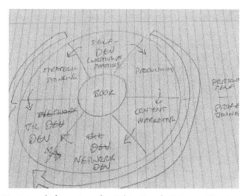

Original drawing for This Book Means Business

This is how I start every significant bit of thinking these days, with the scruffiest piece of blank paper I can lay my hands on. And as you can see I am no Picasso. Luckily you don't need to be either. But Heather goes further: she smartens up her visual thinking and presents her thinking to her readers graphically alongside the text. If you can pull this trick off you win in the battle for attention and understanding.

> *'When you look at text, you turn those texts into symbols that you store in your mind visually. When you look at a picture, you can be something like 30,000 times faster reading all the same information... if [blogs or books] have visuals in them, they are much more often read and understood than if they're just plain text because it breaks it up, it allows you to process things differently.'*

And it *is* a battle, given the astonishing quantity of information that comes at us on a daily basis, demanding our attention – the equivalent of 174 newspapers a day according to Dr Martin Hilbert in 2011.[18] So this shortcut to communicating complex ideas is a powerful competitive advantage for writers who want to be heard.

Over to you

- Try drawing out your ideas for your book as a mind map, a series of interconnected boxes or a shape (a circle, pyramid, arrow etc).
- What do you discover about what you know?
- How could you use this to present your ideas more effectively to your readers?

---

[18] www.martinhilbert.net/WorldInfoCapacity.html/

create distinctive IP

In the Introduction I shared my 'growth curve' model of book writing as business development (and you can see how it's evolved from the original proto-version in **draw out your book** above). It's an original model and it embodies my thinking. If someone wants to use it in future they'll have to credit me. You can't copyright an idea but you automatically have copyright in how you express that idea.

And that's why creating an original model, a distinctive bit of intellectual property, is so significant. Whatever your area of expertise there are almost certainly lots of people talking about it in general terms. Can you be the one to crystallize your ideas into a distinctive, memorable model that becomes a feature on the landscape?

If you can, it will benefit not just your book but your entire business: intellectual property is an asset just as significant as stock in the warehouse and a book is a superb way of asserting and protecting those rights.

Here are just a few examples from Extraordinary Business Book Club guests:

1. Graham Allcott developed the acronym CORD (Capture and Collect, Organize, Review and Do) for his productivity methodology, which also serves as the structural core of his book, so there's a very clear link back into the business and the workshops run by Think Productive.

2. Kelly Pietrangeli based her book on her Project Me productivity and life balance tools, which includes the life wheel she developed first for herself and her friends and then for clients.

3. Nicholas Lovell gave a name and shape to the principle that he was seeing in action and which he'd exploited himself by which free content led to engagement and future spending: The Curve.

4. Amy Wilkinson undertook a massive research project to discover the common practices that underpinned the success of 200 top US entrepreneurs and distilled her findings into the 'Creator's Code', giving each principle a memorable, resonant and distinctive name (my personal favourite is 'Fly the OODA loop').

5. Daniel Priestley wrote *Key Person of Influence* as the cornerstone of a 5-step programme and the book sets out its distinctive alliterative structure: Pitch, Publish, Product, Profile and Partner.

Over to you

- Where's the opportunity for you to create a distinctive bit of intellectual property around your expertise?
- What might that look like?
- How might it inform your products and services as well as your book?

(NB this one will take some time but it might just be the most valuable exercise of the entire book.)

---

start with a proposal

Even if you're planning to self-publish, creating a book proposal is a great place to start because it forces you to think clearly about your book (and by extension your business).

A book proposal is traditionally what you'd submit to an agent or publisher to persuade them to take a punt on your book. It tells them what the book is about, who it's for and why readers will care about any of this. Basically it's the business case for the book: it sets out why this project rather than all the many others being pitched represents a sensible investment of a publisher's time and money.

It also pitches you as the author: are you a desirable business partner? Will you not only write (and, crucially, deliver on time) a good book but will you also be an asset when it comes to marketing and selling it? If nobody knows about you right now, if you're not engaged in and leading the conversation in your area online and off, the publisher could be forgiven for assuming that you're not going to be much help in that department (see **Growing your platform** for more on this).

But YOU need to be clear on this stuff too. Your book represents an investment of your own time and energy and you need to make the business case to yourself.

Here are just a few benefits of working through the proposal process that have nothing at all to do with successfully pitching your proposal to a publisher:

1. You'll get clear on what you're writing about. You may feel you know this already but the discipline of articulating it as a pitch and synopsis – one of

the toughest parts of the 10-day Business Book Proposal Challenge – will force you to strip away the fluff and identify the core of your message. Once you have that it will inform all the marketing you'll ever do, not just your book.

2. Talking about marketing, it'll make you think about that too, right up front, before you might otherwise get round to it. Which is important because how you plan to market your book should inform how you write it and who you involve.

3. Something else you need to get clear on before you start writing is the target reader: exactly who is this book for? And how are they going to recognize it as being something they need in their life? Once you're really clear on whom you're writing for, it becomes much easier to find the appropriate scope, tone of voice and structure (see the **target reader** chapters in **Growing your business** for more on this).

4. Finally one of the most challenging areas for an author to look at dispassionately is competition. It can seem overwhelming: so many books out there already – why should anyone read this one? Well, that's a great question and writing a proposal helps you face it down and find a great answer. Books don't compete with each other in the way that, say, dishwashers do – most readers can't get enough of good books on their favourite topic. Find a distinctive approach or angle, position yourself cleverly in even the most crowded field and competition becomes a reassuring sign of healthy interest in the area, not something to fear.

There are *lots* more specific reasons to write a proposal but maybe it all comes down to this: it gets you started. It's like creating a plan for your building rather than staring at a pile of bricks and wondering what to do with them.

What you do with your finished proposal is up to you. Maybe you just use it as your launch pad and North Star to keep you inspired and on track as you write your book. Maybe you send it to an agent or publisher to pitch for a traditional publishing deal.

But whatever you do, you'll be clearer and more capable and that's not just good for you, it's good for the rest of us too. There are too many poorly thought-through books in the world. Make yours a good one.

Over to you

- You can download a free proposal template from www.thisbookmeansbusinesss.com.
- Fill it in yourself or sign up for the next 10-day Business Book Proposal Challenge (details on the site).

nail your title and subtitle

In one way a title is incredibly important: it's your first and best opportunity to hook the right reader. In another way it doesn't matter at all in the early stages. I find so many authors get hung up on their title, to the point where they can't get on with the writing because they're obsessing about it so much. But in reality the title of a book will often change, sometimes just days before it goes to press, because the focus of the book has shifted in the writing, or because you get some feedback or comment from an early reader that you realize sums it up perfectly. So if all you have right now is a good-enough or working title, that's fine.

Non-fiction books typically have both a title and a subtitle. The title's job is to hook, to capture interest, and the subtitle's job is to explain it and help people find it.

Let's take the subtitle first because it's easier: this is the part that does what it says on the tin and tells the reader exactly what the book's about. Another way of coming at it is to think what someone looking for this information would type into Google. You want them to find this book, after all. Use those words and you've basically just mastered SEO for your book.

Now the title itself and the rule here is: there are no rules.

Seriously.

I guarantee that for every title now considered a classic someone at the editorial meeting didn't like it. The only rule about a great title is that it attracts your **target reader**s. Nobody else has to like it. YOU don't even have to like it. It's no good if you're in love with your title but it doesn't mean much to anyone else. So, even if you think you've nailed it, give yourself permission to think from the ground up for a minute. You might end up with the same title, which is great, and you'll know it works, but you might end up with something completely different.

So how do you get a great title? First, think about the tone of voice and how it fits with your personality, your brand and the way you plan to write the book itself. Is it authoritative, controversial, whimsical, businesslike, mystical, matey, edgy? Find a couple of words that describe the personality you want for your title.

Think too about **metaphors**: getting a metaphor that works as a title is tough; it needs to be original but obvious and it also needs to fit the personality you've identified. Gary Vaynerchuk's *Jab, Jab, Jab, Right Hook: How to Tell Your Story in a Noisy Social World* tells you exactly the approach he's taking and the metaphor is extended throughout the book. If you want to go down this route be prepared to set up a brainstorming board somewhere in your house with a pile of post-its beside it and note down possible ideas as they come to you. Come back to them regularly as you write and see if any might work as a title and even as an organizing principle.

There are a few basic approaches you can take to getting the right title. Michael Hyatt has a useful framework for generating title ideas: PINC – Promise, Intrigue, Need or Content.[19]

Some good examples of **Promise** titles are Dale Carnegie's *How to Win Friends and Influence People*, Joe Wicks's *Lean in 15*, or Tim Ferriss's *The 4-Hour Work Week*:

---

[19] https://michaelhyatt.com/four-strategies-for-creating-titles-that-jump-off-the-page.html

they're basically telling you what you get from reading the book and it has to be pretty damn special. (Notice the last two use assonance and alliteration – more great tricks for making your title stick in people's minds.)

The idea behind **Intrigue** is that you create a question that begs to be answered, for example *The ONE Thing: The Surprisingly Simple Truth Behind Extraordinary Results* by Gary Keller. Michael E. Gerber's *The E-Myth Revisited: Why Most Small Businesses Don't Work and What To Do About It* is another good example. 'E-Myth? What's the E stand for?' – he readily admits most people think it's about technology on first glance – but the subtitle immediately answers the question. As he puts it, the subtitle is the 'translation' of the title.

N for **Need** is one of the most reliable and straightforward approaches: what need does your book meet? These often begin with 'How to', so for example *How to Get to the Top of Google* by Tim Kitchen.

And C for **Content** just sets out what the book's about, basically. *Online Business Startup* by Robin Waite, Wes Linden's *79 Network Marketing Tips* and so on.

There are trends in titles like everything else: one trend I like at the moment, and which I think won't date too badly, is the single word title. Malcolm Gladwell is a master of this: *Outliers*, *Blink* and so on. These look great on a thumbnail but it's unlikely you'll be able to own the .com URL and you'll have to make the subtitle do all the heavy lifting in explaining what the book's about and who it's for.

If you can create a portmanteau title by joining two concepts together you can get the best of all worlds: it's short, memorable and distinctive. It's also very hard to do. Malcolm Durham did this beautifully with *WealthBeing* and the classic example, of course, is *Freakonomics* by Steven Levitt and Stephen Dubner.

Finally, there's a couple of hygiene issues to consider when you choose your title:

1. **Spelling**. If you're after an international audience it's always good to avoid words that are spelled differently in the UK and US, like 'color' or 'center' or 'mom'. And if you're using words that are challenging to spell, such as 'millennium' or 'fluorescent', you may miss out on some search results.

2. **Length**. Most people's first view of your cover will be as a thumbnail image so you need to make sure they can comfortably read the title at 80 x 115 pixels. If it's long there's unlikely to be space for an image so make sure you're OK with that. Even if the title is only one word long, if that's a very long word, it may be difficult to read at a small size (unless you hyphenate it). Generally, shorter is better.

3. **Availability**. You can't trademark a title so it's not illegal to call your book the same as another one, but you could come up against a legal challenge if it can be shown you're deliberately trying to create confusion between them. And honestly, why would you want to do that anyway? That's just going to annoy your readers. Check on Amazon and if your title's close to another book's think how you can make it distinctive. Also, check if the URL for your title is available and if it is, buy it. You don't have to set up a separate site – you can redirect it to

a book page on your existing site if you choose –
but it keeps your options open and stops someone
else using it. (And if someone is already using it,
particularly if they're in your field, think hard about
choosing that phrase as your title: do you want to
risk sending people there?)

Over to you

- Identify your title's personality in one or two
  words, remembering it has to appeal to your
  ideal (**target) reader**) and it also has to fit
  with your own personality online and off to be
  consistent and authentic.
- Spend half an hour or so brainstorming your
  title – get down as many as you can, be playful
  and inventive; if you find a metaphor or phrase
  you like riff with it, use it as a stepping stone
  to something else. Quantity breeds quality. You
  can think about your subtitle too but focus on
  that primary hook.
- Choose one to go with as your working title –
  and if you're really happy with it buy the URL!

write a summary

A literary agent once told me: 'If you can't describe your book in two sentences, you're in trouble.' Not only will you find it hard to sell your book, you'll struggle to write it, because you're not really clear what you're trying to achieve.

Brevity isn't easy. (Witness Blaise Pascale: 'I would have written a shorter letter but I did not have the time.') So try starting with a longer overview – no more than three paragraphs or so. In the first one focus on what the book's about, who it's for and what it does for them, in the second outline how it does what it does, and in the third explain why you're the right person to write this book and any other points that will grab a reader's attention.

Basically you're answering these three questions: what? so what? and who cares?

If even that's too hard take a step further back: describe your book as fully as you like to help you clarify it for yourself. Look at what you've written and identify the really important bits. Then rewrite it more succinctly; this can be the version you use on your own website for warm leads.

Revisit that a few days later and see what can be taken out without losing the essential points – take it down to that three-paragraph overview. Then finally distil that down into your pitch, the two-sentence (or even one-sentence) hook that sums it up without a single wasted word.

If you need inspiration take a look at Amazon and see how the bestselling books in your area do it: Steve Peters, *The Chimp Paradox*, has a good overview and a punchy one-sentence summary: '*The Chimp Paradox* is an incredibly powerful mind management model that can help you become a happy, confident, healthier and more successful person.'

And here's Eric Ries's summary: '*The Lean Startup* is a new approach to business that's being adopted around the world. It is changing the way companies are built and new products are launched. *The Lean Startup* is about learning what your customers really want. It's about testing your vision continuously, adapting and adjusting before it's too late.'

And here's one of the shortest I've ever seen, from Fiona Humberstone, author of *How to Style your Brand*: 'Everything you need to know to create a distinctive brand identity.'

Writing a summary is really hard to do. But you'll be glad you did.

Over to you

- Start at whatever point you feel comfortable – summary, overview or long description – and work back to create that one- or two-sentence summary.
- Try it out on **target reader**s: does it work to engage their interest and get them excited? If not, take the learnings and go through the process again.

decide how long your book will be

Why is it important to decide on length up front? Why not just start writing and see where you finish?

1. Because you may never finish. There's always more to say and, if you don't know what you're aiming for, how are you going to know when you get there?
2. Because if you end up writing a 100,000-word book it may be so expensive to produce that you'll have to price it too high and/or limit the number of free copies you can afford to give out.
3. Because once you know how long you want it to be you can start breaking that down to get the balance between the different sections right. See '**structure – create a framework**'.

What's the right length for your book?

There's no hard and fast rule but this one is around 55,000 words and if I'd had more self-discipline I'd have trimmed it to 45,000. If you're over 60,000 words for a business book it might be time for the blue pencil. Less is more.

For the standard business book format, 5.5 x 8.5 inches or 216 x 138 millimetres, you'll get about 200 to 300 words per page depending on spacing, subheads and so on. Add 16 pages or so for prelims and endmatter, allow for any illustrations and you can roughly calculate how many pages that equates to. Under 100 pages and you'll struggle to be able to print the title on the spine; over 300 pages and you're demanding a serious commitment from your reader

– and if you're paying the production costs yourself you'll be sharing that pain.

Bernadette Jiwa writes brilliant books. Books like *Difference*, *Marketing: A Love Story* and *Hunch*. And one of the first things you notice about them is that they're very short. Beautifully, enticingly, 'it-would-be-so-easy-to-read-this' short. I asked her about it.

'I go into bookshops all of the time, and I watch people buying books, or actually more browsing books and putting them back, and I would encourage you, if you're a writer, to go and do this. You can see people weighing a book in their hands... They flick through the first few pages, they look at the cover, and then they think, "I haven't got time for this."... I said, "OK, how can I write books that people will read all the way to the end, they can open at any page and find something interesting or useful or inspiring or actionable, and they'll come back to it again?" That's my intention for the books, because the people I write for are busy people.'

We're all busy. You're busy. That's why I wrote this book as a series of short chapters you can dip in and out of. And guess what: your readers? They're busy too.

Over to you

- Decide how long you want your book to be in words.
- Work out roughly how many pages that equates to.

---

structure – do the thinking

'I'm always saying to writers when they start out – and they seem to want to ignore me but I'll keep saying it – focus on getting the structure and the proposal right. It's like painting a room. The hard bit is masking everything off and moving all the furniture out and putting down the dustsheets and all that stuff and then painting it is quite easy…. With a book a lot of people struggle because they start writing, because they think a book is all about writing, and then they get to the critical point and they suddenly realize "I've got to start again, the structure isn't right, I haven't really thought this through, I've written myself into a hole that I can't get out of," and they get disheartened.' – Matt Watkinson

One of the most consistent bits of advice from successful authors in the Extraordinary Business Book Club is to start with the structure.

When you can pull all your disparate ideas into a coherent whole – when the pieces of your argument and evidence fall into place and flow naturally to the conclusion you've been trying to articulate, when the balance between sections is right and you can give your reader clear and consistent signposts to help them navigate through your content and identify the piece they need to read *right now* – it's a beautiful thing. And it doesn't happen by accident. You need a carefully measured blend of divergent and convergent thinking and a dash of discipline.

So where do you start? For the divergent thinking phase I suggest a free-form mind map. Don't just write your ideas down tamely on an A4 piece of paper: use post-it notes and as much wall space as you can commandeer over a period of a few days. Scribble each thought or topic on a separate post-it, with as much detail as you can manage (you'll be surprised how quickly you forget what that cryptic single word meant), stick them on the wall and keep turning things over in your mind while you run, shower, sort laundry – whenever you're engaged in one of those occupations that allows your mind to drift unhindered. (Agatha Christie suggested the best time for planning a book was while doing the dishes.)

Don't try and close things down prematurely – keep your mind open and accepting, keep coming up with ideas and letting the ideas you've already had generate more in their turn. If you can manage a week in this expansive, exploratory phase so much the better.

Once the ideas have dried up it's time to start with the convergent thinking. Stand back and take a long, hard look at what you've got. Start moving post-its around to group related concepts together (this is where you'll be thankful you didn't just write on a sheet of paper). This is contents-page planning from the ground up: the clusters you identify will become your chapter or section headings and there will almost certainly be a natural sequence or logic to help you order them.

There will also probably be outliers – ideas that aren't quite right for this book. Don't lose these – stick them in a 'pending' file to be used as blog posts, marketing campaigns, interviews or even a future book.

Once you've mapped out what's going to be in your book and roughly how it will be organized, you can take it to the next step and turn it into a **working table of contents**.

Over to you

- Use the post-it technique – or another method if you prefer – to brainstorm what your book will cover and how the ideas relate to each other.
- What overall shape and scope emerges?
- What questions does this process raise and how will you go about answering them?

structure – create a framework

Once you've done the big thinking about your structure it's time to pull it together into a form that you can use as the framework for your book.

In my editorial career I've worked on many multi-contributor reference books, which had to be carefully structured before the writing began. I worked alongside the editor(s) to define an overarching set of macro categories, the broad areas that we wanted the book to cover. Then we'd decide on the overall balance of the book, what proportion of the total should be given to each area, to give a high-level, top-down allocation of words, before allocating a word length to each individual article. This is essential when you're about to commission 1,000+ contributors but it's a great way to plan any non-fiction book.

If you decide your book on running will be 50,000 words, for example, your macro categories – or parts, or sections or chapters – might include technique, kit, nutrition, injury prevention and training plans. Giving equal weight to each of these means you'd have 10,000 words for each area but you might decide the technique section is so complex that it requires 25% of the book (12,500 words) in which case you'd adjust another section (or sections) downwards to compensate.

Within each section there are likely to be subsections, which might correspond to individual chapters or to subheadings, so for example nutrition might break down into hydration, pre-run fuelling, fuelling while running, post-run fuelling, and general diet. Again you will need to decided the appropriate balance between each of these and assign your words accordingly: if there are 10,000 words available for this chapter and you allocate them evenly between these subheadings you know you have 2,000 words in which to say everything you want to say about hydration.

Here's what that might look like if you take the hierarchy approach:

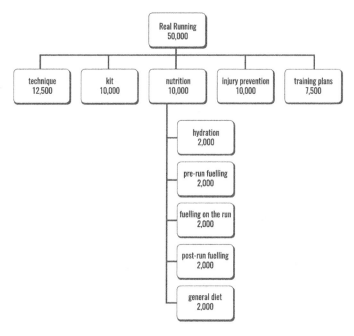

Hierachy approach

And if you prefer mind maps, it might look more like this:

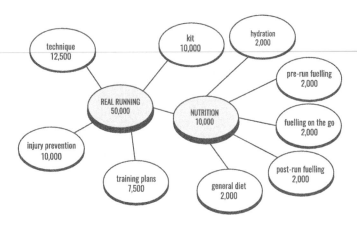

Mind map approach

Control freakery? Well, maybe. But the big advantage of starting in this top-down fashion is that you are far less likely to lose your way when you start writing: you know exactly what you plan to cover in each section and roughly how many words to spend on each. The bigger the book, the more complex the topic, the more people involved in the writing, the more useful the hierarchy becomes.

And if it becomes clear you have too much to say and not enough words in which to say it, better to know sooner rather than later. Maybe there are actually two books here, even a whole **series in disguise**?

This top-down approach also helps you identify structural elements – for example, case studies – and establish a consistent format for them (e.g. heading, summary, narrative, key point). That consistency helps the reader know what to expect and where to find key information. It also helps you avoid presenting similar information in different ways for no good reason, a sure way to confuse and irritate your readers.

Over to you

- Identify the macro categories for your book and sketch out a hierarchy or mind map, ideally down to at least chapter level. You'll probably want to have several goes at this but, once you've got it right, this will be one of the single most effective tools to help you write the book well and – crucially – to know when it's complete.
- Take a look at some of the books you admire and notice how they're structured: what works and what doesn't work so well? What do you find particularly useful or interesting as a reader? What can you learn or use for your own book?

structure – working table of contents

Getting your book's structure right is the first step towards a well-put-together contents page, which matters more than you might think: it's front and centre in the Amazon preview of your book and perhaps the single most powerful element in the buy/bye decision.

If your table of contents, or TOC, shows a clear, well-thought-through and consistent structure the reader will take this as a signal that the book itself is clear and well thought through, and trust you to guide them through the material. A long list of chapter headings makes them think they're on their own and that you're not going to help them make sense of all this stuff, at which point they will possibly lose the will to live and almost certainly the will to read.

So your TOC needs to reflect your structure but it also needs to convey your meaning and ideally something of your personality. The clearer you can be in the headings you use, the more the reader will be able to see the value of the content – it's a taster of what's to come.

Before you get to that stage, however, you can create a working TOC, a living document that's a tool primarily for you, the writer. This will be your best friend throughout the writing process, because when you sit down to write you'll have absolutely clarity on what you're going to write about and how it fits into the bigger picture. And it's a great way to track your progress.

Your working TOC will drill down deeper than the kind at the front of books: it will include subheadings – maybe even bullet points showing what you're going to cover and in what order – and it may include the word count for each element so you can track the writing as you go.

Another useful way to use the working TOC is to set out any repeating structural elements within each chapter. Will you start each chapter with a quote, for example, or a story that illustrates a particular problem? Will you finish with a bullet point summary of your key points or a set of questions for the reader to consider? Will you sprinkle tips or tools or references to other resources through the text? These won't go into the final TOC seen by the reader but it's useful to include them in your working TOC so that you see how they fit with the other elements and ensure you've allowed enough words for them.

Over to you

From the structural work you've done so far:

- Create a working TOC for your book using Excel, Word, Scrivener or whichever method you prefer.
- Include any repeating structural elements and the word count for each item.

MAKING IT HAPPEN

So far we've done a lot of warming the teapot: now it's time to make the tea. How can you get started and keep going with the act of writing now you're ready to make it happen?

In this section we look in detail at how to design a writing routine that works for you, including tools to help you organize your research and practical tips for developing your writing habit.

Louise Wiles, author of *Thriving Abroad*, told me that organizing her research was the hardest part for her:

> *'I wrote scrappy notes in various notebooks and created content for the book using vague references, then when it came to the final draft I was scrabbling around looking for the full references and links... I got there in the end but I could have saved myself a lot of time and frustration.'*[20]

So that's where we begin this section: with a selection of tools to help you organize the mountain of online and offline material that feeds into your book.

---

[20] Email conversation, March 2017.

organize your research – the commonplace book

This is one of the oldest research tools for writers. A commonplace book is essentially a scrapbook, a compilation of whatever bits and pieces the compiler found interesting. They started to become popular in the 17th century and by the 18th century no scholar worth his salt was without one. They're usually thought of as writers' tools but in fact their use was much broader: yes, Michel de Montaigne collected quotations and ideas that appealed to him in his commonplace book but Linnaeus also used one as he formed his system of species classifications; even Sherlock Holmes had one to help him solve crimes.

This isn't journaling or keeping a diary, valuable though they both are: it's clipping and collecting. It's not the output of your thinking; it's the raw input.

If you prefer to work with physical material rather than keep notes online, this might be a good solution for you. Find a good-sized notebook and write your notes and references, together with your observations and the date, directly into it, or use a lever arch file and insert handwritten notes and printed pages – this also allows you to reorder things more easily.

One benefit of writing out notes longhand like this is that the act of writing triggers deeper memory and commitment.

Mark Levy spoke in the Extraordinary Business Book Club about the importance of collecting your 'fascination pile' as a starting point for your book and this is another aspect of that: collecting unrelated elements and then sifting back through them, picking out the patterns and relationships to create something new and significant.

There's nothing commonplace about this kind of purposeful, curious curation, sadly. But getting a system in place – creating the space for it – is a good first step. Then go about your day knowing that when you hit upon gold you have a place to store it.

Over to you

If the idea of a commonplace book appeals to you experiment with how to do it.

- Will you use a book or a file?
- What size works best?
- Will you write out passages longhand or simply make notes and include a reference so you can look up the original?

organize your research – index cards

Ryan Holiday is a commonplace book enthusiast but he's also blogged in detail about the way he uses index cards in his research and writing,[21] adapted from the system taught to him by Robert Greene.

Index cards are a fabulous low-tech writer's tool. You can always have a few with you since they take up almost no space at all; they work offline and don't need recharging, they force you to write concisely (but not TOO concisely – there's space for a few sentences), they can be coded with any classification system of your choice along the top, and they can be re-ordered at your leisure.

Just the physical act of writing out and organizing the cards can create a breakthrough in your thinking, as Tim Harford discovered in the process of using them as prompts for a talk while he was writing his book *Adapt*:

> *'As I was writing out the 3×5 inch cards… I realized, "This chapter's in the wrong order." (I'd been working on this chapter for months.) "Why on earth would you start a chapter where you've started it? Whereas in fact you should be starting it with this thing that is 3– or 4,000 words in, and if you start there, then you hook people's attention and then you get them to understand what really the problem is."'*

---

[21] See https://ryanholiday.net/the-notecard-system-the-key-for-remembering-organizing-and-using-everything-you-read/ for more details.

As Tim demonstrates, index cards are also useful tools for helping you structure and deliver talks. They worked brilliantly for me as note-taking and revision tools when I was studying for my MBA: I found that the secret was to give each card a title and then above that, along the very top of the card, add two or three keywords, one being the main category under which it would be filed. I also made sure I added full references if I was quoting or citing a source, after a couple of frustrating hours spent trying to locate the reference to a quote I wanted to use in an essay.

Over to you

If the idea of index cards appeals to you experiment with how to use them.

- What size works best?
- How will you store them?
- What categories will you use?
- Will you write out passages longhand or simply make notes and include a reference so you can look up the original?

organize your research – online tools

If the thought of using such low-tech tools leaves you cold there are plenty of online, cloud-based equivalents you can turn to. The advantages here of course are that you can access them wherever you are (assuming you have an internet connection). They'll also never get lost or damaged; you can use as many tags as you like and sort by any one of them any time you like; you'll always be able to read the writing, and you can simply pin or paste material rather than laboriously writing it out by hand. (Although, as I note above, that's also a disadvantage: the act of writing makes it more likely you'll remember something and engage actively with it – how many times have you casually highlighted or bookmarked a quote and never thought of it again?)

Here are just a few of the tools used by members of the Extraordinary Business Book Club and/or authors who've appeared on the podcast (see the **Useful tools** section at the end of the book for more details):

Evernote – this is my personal favourite. As simple as it needs to be, but no simpler, and it allows me to include written or audio notes.

Google Docs – Michael Bhaskar, author of *Curation*, uses this and he knows a thing or two about curating material.

Google Keep – recommended by EBBC member Linda Scannell.

Trello – I love this for task management but Kelly Pietrangeli swears by it for organizing ideas for her book too.

Pinterest – useful for collecting web pages and particularly images.

Blogging tools, eg WordPress – for a private (or indeed public) blog.

Pocket – not one I've used myself but several EBBC members swear by it.

Scrivener – this is a fabulous tool not just for research but for writing (it allows you to track your progress against goals, for example, which I find very motivating). There is a bit of a learning hump but if you can get over that it might just become your favourite writing tool of all.

But you don't need to get to grips with a new system if you don't want to: sometimes the simplest ideas are the best. Tony Crabbe, author of *Busy*, organizes his research by putting everything interesting into a folder on his computer.

'I tend to read electronically because I travel a lot so I don't really store things in paper versions, only electronically. I set up this file folder ages ago called "personal learnings" and under that I've got tons and tons of different headings for different topics. When I find a great academic article or an interesting blog

post or whatever, I'll just save it into those so they become a more and more useful resource for me to draw on. When I'm working on a book or on a project, I keep Word documents which are just a collection of anything that feels relevant – ideas, thoughts, reflections on stories get dumped into those... just "see page 76 this book", or "check out this TED talk". Then it becomes a progressive part of the research phase of the book, going through those and organizing them into something meaningful.'

Over to you

If the idea of using an online tool appeals to you take a look at the examples above.

- Which looks like it might suit you best?
- How could you try it out?
- Think about how you'll structure the tool to reflect the chapters or themes of your book.

develop your writing habit – find your space

When Graham Allcott realized he wasn't getting round to finishing his book *How to Be A Productivity Ninja* (oh, the irony) he reengineered his business so someone else could run it and took himself off to a beach hut in Sri Lanka for a month to focus exclusively on the book. Sadly, a beach hut isn't an option for most of us but, as Graham points out, 'your Sri Lanka might be a coffee shop for an hour' – the point is to separate yourself from the normal business of life and give yourself time, space and permission to focus on the writing.

For me, writing at home at my usual desk simply doesn't work. It may be quiet but there are endless silent distractions: the invoice that needs processing, an email demanding an answer, the washing that needs hanging out. I did most of the writing for this book elsewhere: in Basingstoke library, on Extraordinary Business Book Club writing days, house-sitting in Devon with a friend, holed up on my own in an Airbnb cottage.

Try different places at different times – as an extrovert, I find having people around helps me relax into the writing but introverts may need silence and solitude. It's getting harder and harder to find that in public libraries but if you live near a university consider getting a 'reference-only' access pass: university libraries always have quiet spaces available, usually on the upper floors.

If you can, though, find a spot at home away from your usual business desk that works for you and make it your writing space. That way it's always available to you and your brain will quickly learn that when you're sitting here, you're writing.

And when you've found your writing groove, and it's locked to that writing place, find a way to take it with you whenever you have to be away. Melissa Romo has a small frog that sits atop her writing desk at home and which accompanies her whenever she has to travel.

'If I know I can't write from my desk, I carry the frog, I put it in my purse, and when I'm in the new space that's not my usual space, I pull the frog out, and it's almost a way to cue myself, as if I were at my desk.'

Over to you

- Where can you create a space to write that's away from your usual place of work?
- Try writing in a completely new place: a coffee shop, a library, a gallery, wherever. What do you notice?
- What could work as your 'frog' to cue your brain to write even if you're on the other side of the world?

develop your writing habit - piggyback on what's already there

Your life is already full of habits. You don't need to use willpower to brush your teeth: you probably don't even really think about it. Bathroom jobs (as they're known in our house) are embedded into your morning and evening routines. So use the incredibly strong power of the habits you already have and make them work for the new writing habit you're trying to create.

Behaviour scientist B. J. Fogg has done some fascinating research in this area. He suggests starting with something that's already part of your day and grafting onto it a small, doable new habit (he calls them 'tiny habits') so that you set yourself up for success. He has used the technique in his own life: in his TEDx talk[22] he reveals how he began introducing a push-up every time he went to the bathroom. Over time he increased that number until finally he was doing 70 push-ups a day.

If you're trying to establish a new writing routine, think about how you can create a new tiny habit. If you always make a coffee after you've dropped the kids at school, for example, introduce a notebook and take five minutes to write or plan your writing while you drink it. Make it automatic and you overcome one of the biggest barriers to creating a new habit, that of motivation.

Bec Evans of Prolifiko put it this way:

'Make a task so small you can't put it off… If you want to start writing just say to yourself, "I'm just

---

[22] https://youtu.be/AdKUJxjn-R8

going to pick up my notepad and I'm just going to write down my title and two words." Then you do that one day and then the next day you think, "I'm just going to spend another minute doing this."… We call it writing unthinkingly, so not relying on your willpower, which depletes as you go through the day.'

Over to you

If you need to start your writing habit:

- What tiny habit could you establish?
- What existing habit could you piggyback that on?

develop your writing habit - streaking

In common parlance a streaker is someone who strips naked and runs – usually very fast, hence 'streaking' – across a public space for reasons best known to themselves. Maybe they're trying to protest about something or maybe they just don't know when to say no to a dare.

Whatever way you look at it, streakers are all in. They're committed. (And sometimes they end up committed, too.)

For runners streaking has a slightly different meaning: going for a run every day. The most famous streaker in this sense of the word is Ron Hill, who ran every day from December 1964 until he stopped aged 78 in January 2017. He ran with a broken sternum, on walking sticks after bunion surgery, even with his leg in a cast. And it certainly worked for him: all his best race performances came after he'd started streaking: 'Once you get into the habit of it,' he said, 'you just do it.'

Another famous streaker who keeps his clothes on – at least I assume he does – is Seth Godin. He's blogged since 2002 and for most of those years he's blogged every day. Some posts are long, most are short.

'It's a discipline, it requires rigour, it's scary, which are three of the things that are good about it… It requires you to put your name on your thought. It leaves a trail. If you know that every day, day after day, 365 days a year, you're going to be leaving a trail about ideas, about culture, about the work you think that matters, I can't help but imagine that you will think about it a little more deeply…. That is a wonderful gift to the blogger regardless of whether anyone reads it or not.'

Inspired by both of these, I blogged and ran every day for a year and discovered something magical: when you have to do something every day there's no willpower involved. It's not 'Will I blog today?' it's 'When will I blog today?'

Jerry Seinfeld famously used this principle too. He hung a calendar on his wall with a red marker pen beside it then, every day he wrote, he put a big 'X' over the date.

'After a few days you'll have a chain. Just keep at it and the chain will grow longer every day. You'll like seeing that chain, especially when you get a few weeks under your belt. Your only job next is to not break the chain.' [23]

Streaking isn't for everyone, and it will almost certainly mean that some days you don't produce your best stuff, but it is a powerful way of making sure that you come up with *something* and at least then you're in the game.

Over to you

If streaking appeals to you, think about how you could try it out.

- Could you set yourself the goal of writing every day for a month?
- What will be your minimum output (100 words? 500 words? 1,000 words?)? Sarah Arrow's 30-day blogging challenge on Facebook is a great place to start.

---

[23] As reported by Brad Isaac: http://lifehacker.com/281626/jerry-seinfelds-productivity-secret

develop your writing habit – overcoming writer's block

Much of this book is aimed at overcoming writer's block in one way or another – that feeling of inertia and emptiness as you stare at the page in front of you and realize you got nothing – but it seemed only right to include a chapter tackling it head on.

Alan Weiss, author of *Breaking Through Writer's Block*, takes a muscular approach to the problem:

> 'There's no such thing as writer's block. It's a myth. What you do is you sit down at a keyboard and you type a letter, and then you type some more letters, you have a word. Then you type some more words, you have a sentence. A few more sentences, you have a paragraph. What you write is better than you think, but what stops people is the self-editing, this little person in your head who keeps critiquing you. You got to kill that person, you just got to flick them off your shoulder, stomp on them 'til they're bloody. You have to sit down and write, and stop worrying whether people will like it. Just write for yourself.'

Joanna Penn suggests that writer's block often reflects the fact that you can't output good stuff without good input:

> 'I think a lot of the time writer's block is [they] have not filled their creative well enough. You have to put stuff in your head, however you do that, reading,

watching films... Especially with non fiction, if you haven't got enough personal anecdotes then go out and do some stuff... go and do something that you can then bring back and use in your book.'

And Seth Godin, in his blog, argues that if you view writing like talking the problem goes away.

'No one ever gets talker's block. No one wakes up in the morning, discovers he has nothing to say and sits quietly, for days or weeks, until the muse hits, until the moment is right, until all the craziness in his life has died down.

Why then, is writer's block endemic?

The reason we don't get talker's block is that we're in the habit of talking without a lot of concern for whether or not our inane blather will come back to haunt us. Talk is cheap. Talk is ephemeral. Talk can be easily denied.

We talk poorly and then, eventually (or sometimes), we talk smart. We get better at talking precisely because we talk. We see what works and what doesn't, and if we're insightful, do more of what works. How can one get talker's block after all this practice?

Writer's block isn't hard to cure.

Just write poorly. Continue to write poorly, in public, until you can write better.'[24]

For what it's worth, I've found the two most powerful ways to overcome writer's block is to help my authors (and indeed myself):

1. Get clear on who you're writing for and why.
2. Break down the book into manageable chunks.

As Grace Marshall put it:

'If you have "write book" on your to-do list, it's just never going to get done. It's huge. We tend to procrastinate over the stuff that's big, boring, or scary. "Write book" is definitely big and scary, so find ways of breaking it down.'

Over to you

- Do you suffer from writer's block? If so, try each of these approaches in turn until you find one that unblocks you.

team up

One of the most treasured memories of my publishing career is a weekend spent in snowy upstate New York, near the Sleepy Hollow of Washington Irving's famous legend. An energetic and visionary general editor had managed to secure funding for his team of specialist editors and me, the in-house editor, to spend the weekend getting a new major reference work off to a flying start.

On the first day we introduced ourselves, he spoke about his vision for the book, I explained the process for creating it and the team discussed both at length. The next day we hammered out the framework: the balance between the sections, the key topics and the relationships between them, how we would handle problematic areas – from historiological controversy to non-responsive contributors – and so on.

I'm sure it's no coincidence that this was one of the smoothest projects I ever worked on: it was delivered on schedule and to the correct extent – no small achievement for a book of around 500,000 words – and the quality was uniformly superb.

I've often thought, though, that the real magic happened below the surface, not just in the discussions themselves: in the coffee breaks and over dinner and in the shared experience of Tarrytown in its winter splendour we quietly built up relationships based on mutual liking and respect, becoming part of each other's personal and professional network for years afterwards. Throughout the actual writing of the book the editorial team members were constantly in touch with each other. It would have been unthinkable for one to let the others down.

Sadly, not every writer can afford the luxury of a weekend in Tarrytown with a team of like-minded individuals but, no matter what your situation, there's no excuse for trying to do everything alone in the 21st century.

Writing works best with a bit of creative friction. You need other people's oddly shaped ideas to bounce off if you're to keep momentum and find new directions, and you almost certainly need someone checking in with you if you're to have any chance of hitting a deadline. Writing alone is like drinking alone: it's OK, but you don't want to be doing too much of it.

Here are a few ideas to get you out of your garret and into the bracing embrace of others, who can help you not only get your book written but make it better:

1. **Find a friend**. Do you know anyone else who's in the throes of writing a book? #amwriting is a useful hashtag to search on Twitter; you might be surprised to find some of your Twitter buddies already using it. Why not buddy up – even a monthly call to report in with each other on progress and talk through knotty issues can be helpful.

2. **Join an online community**. There's the Extraordinary Business Book Club, of course, but we're not the only show in town: try NaNonFiWriMo or find a LinkedIn or Facebook group: look around, find a place that feels homey, pull up a chair and get involved.

3. **Join a programme**. A step up from simply joining a community, and significantly more likely to provide the results you want, a small-group programme is a more focused and supportive way to combine the

benefits of working with others with the direction of an expert. Especially if this is your first book, there is likely to be much that you don't know you don't know: a small-group programme such as my bootcamp is part therapy, part training, part coaching.

4.   **Get a coach or mentor**. This is the gold standard. It's particularly important if your book is intended to build your business: investing in a specialist writing or publishing coach who will work with you to clarify exactly what you should be focusing on and how to link it to your business activities will avoid you wasting precious time and energy on an ineffectual end product. And nobody does accountability like a coach – trust me on this.

Over to you

- Which of these ways of teaming up appeals most to you?
- What could you do today to take the first step towards making it happen?

talk it out

Sometimes, writing isn't the best way to write a book.

Robin Waite was a busy man. He was running his own business building websites and developing online business strategy for an ever-growing list of customers. At home, he was doing his bit looking after a 3-month-old baby. So when he decided to write a book, the obvious question was: when? Robin's solution was to plan out in detail the structure of his book (see **Working table of contents**) and then dictate it, one commute at a time.

> 'On my journey into work, I used to record for about 15 minutes. I'd choose a chapter, do 5 bullets per chapter, talk about each bullet in 2 minutes, so I'd have 10 minutes per chapter recorded, and then during my lunch break I actually sat down and transcribed it myself, and post-edited it.'

There are two big reasons why dictating is a great way to write a book:

1. **Speed.** It took Robin around six weeks to write two of his bestselling books (*Online Business Start-up* and *Take Your Shot*) using this method and, as an added bonus, the fact that he took the opportunity to clarify his thoughts and polish the text during the post-editing meant the book was 'pretty much good to go' when it arrived with the publisher. Most of us can talk faster than we can type (around 100 words per minute – I don't know what your typing speed is but mine's certainly nowhere near

that). And sometimes the friction involved in typing can slow us down to the point where we lose the freshness and intensity of our thinking, which leads me to the second advantage of dictating your book...

2. **Tone of voice**. Speaking out loud means quite literally speaking in your own voice, and if you imagine you're speaking to your **target reader** it can be much easier to hit the right tone. As readers we want to feel as though the author's talking directly to us and talking the book out rather than writing onto a blank screen can help with that.

This is a particularly useful technique for those for whom writing doesn't come easily. (And why should it? Just because you're great at what you do doesn't mean you're necessarily great at writing about it.)

It's also a useful trick to try if you're writing the traditional way but get stuck, or you find your message disappearing under the weight of big words and highfalutin language: stand up, move about, imagine your reader by your side and simply tell them what you have to say, with the voice-recorder app running unobtrusively in the background.

You don't have to transcribe yourself, as Robin did; dictation tools such as Dragon or online transcription services like Rev.com are great alternatives to speed things up.

Over to you

- Take one of the bullet points from your TOC and try speaking rather than writing what you want to say.
- You can either record and transcribe yourself, making changes as you go, or use a tool such as Dragon or a service like Rev.com and review the transcript.
- Does it feel like a better route to create your book than sitting and writing the traditional way? If so, set up your systems and crack on!

read it out loud

My kids still love being read to. Even the 14-year-old. They're perfectly capable of reading books for themselves these days – and do, voraciously – but there's still something wonderful about the ritual of reading together.

Picture books are designed to be read aloud and the best, like Julia Donaldson's, have a music and rhythm in the words that's irresistible as you read. They're also memorable: we're way past *A Squash and a Squeeze* now but I can still pretty much recite the whole book from memory (I know because I just tried).

With the chapter books we read now, though, there are occasional moments when I stumble as I read. Sometimes it's a clumsy repetition, or a bit of dialogue that doesn't reveal it's a question until the end when it's too late to inflect correctly, or even a grammatical error. There's something about reading aloud that exposes the writing in a way that skimming it silently in your head fails to do.

And that's why it's so helpful (and occasionally excruciating) to read your own writing out loud. This is a great technique to use at any time, but particularly towards the end of the editing process, when the text is pretty much there and you're happy with the structure and stories you're using to make your points.

Here are just a few of the issues I've discovered for myself when I read my own writing aloud, in addition to the more obvious issues such as typos and grammatical errors:

- **I've lost the tone.** There's a tendency when you write to use big words and a more formal register, and only when you read it back do you realize you sound like a pompous twit. Better for you to discover that now and fix it than to hear it from your readers.

- **I overuse some words.** This will not come as a surprise to regular listeners. 'Lovely', 'great', 'really', 'just' – they rarely add anything, and there's never an excuse for three in one paragraph.
- **I've lost the point**. The sentence might have known where it was going when it started out but then it took a detour and never recovered. Reading aloud forces me to notice that I've left an idea unfinished.
- **It just doesn't sound right**. I'm fairly clued up on the mechanics, what with having a degree in English Language, but you don't need that to know when something just sounds wrong. Native speakers know massively more about their language than they could ever put into words. You know how to order adjectives, for example (quantity, quality, size, age, shape, colour, nationality, qualifier: 'the second lovely big old square dark-brown French writing desk') but I bet you couldn't explain why. If it sounds wrong to you, it will sound wrong to your reader, so go with your instincts.
- **The pace is wrong**. Usually it's too slow or there aren't enough breaks. I go back and take out words and add full stops and paragraph breaks until it feels friendlier and more natural.

If you don't believe me, believe Seth Godin:

'If you can't read the first chapter out loud, then you're writing the wrong way. The good news is, the solution is super easy. If it was the opposite, this would be really hard. If it was, "This sounds too much like you," then I don't know how to teach you to sound like someone else.'

Michael Neill is a big believer in this process too; it helps him discover what he calls 'the music of the book':

'For my final edit I read the book out loud, partly because I go snow blind, I just can't see it on the page any more, but also because then I can hear the conversation in it.'[25]

Over to you

After you've written a few hundred words, try reading them back to yourself.

- What do you notice?
- What can you change about the way you write to make it sound better out loud?

---

[25] In conversation, July 2015.

reward yourself

If you've ever trained a dog, you'll know that obedience is powered by rewards. We're not so different. Ever walked up and down stairs twice before bedtime just to hit your target and get the 'Good job!' message from your activity tracker?

Rewards (OK, bribes) can be a powerful way to help you establish a writing habit too. Bec Evans explains:

> *'Behaviour change is all about that dopamine hit… If you're training yourself to do something you need to reward yourself as well. Often it starts off being something external. "If I finish this 200 words I'm going to spend 5 minutes on Facebook." Whatever you think your reward is. It could just be a really nice cup of coffee. What's really important is having very small rewards for small progress. It's not like, "I've done 250 words. I'm going to have a bottle of champagne." You'll never get your book finished at that rate.'*

(Though we agreed you could have a lot of fun trying.)

Grace Marshall, author of *How to be Really Productive*, points out that one of the reasons writing is so hard is that it works on a different reward scale to the one we've grown used to. We check our phones tens, maybe hundreds, of times each day and we're regularly rewarded by that dopamine hit: a new like, a comment, an email.

> *'Writing is a very deep-dive activity… A lot of what we do in today's life and today's world of work is scanning – checking emails, running from one meeting to another, Facebook, Twitter – all of that stuff is really*

quick hits, and from a productivity point of view, when you're so used to getting quick hits, writing a book is completely different.'

You may find that the thought of your book in your hands at the end of it all and the intrinsic interest of the writing process is reward enough but, for most of us, setting smaller, more tangible goals just tantalizingly out of reach is a big help in getting us to the keyboard.

Over to you

What rewards could you give yourself to help keep your motivation high?

- You might want to consider tiny rewards, such as 5 minutes Facebooking after 25 minutes writing, and bigger ones, such as a takeaway when you've finished a chapter.
- Maybe go crazy and plan a fabulous reward for when you finish the entire first draft (for me it was a fish-and-chip supper and most of a bottle of Prosecco).

create a writing playlist

Personally, I find it hard to write with music in the background. But I *do* write better with an ambient hum of other people's noise around me. For many music has a similar function: a 'white noise' that allows them to focus more effectively than complete silence, particularly when they're wearing noise-cancelling headphones that cut down on external distractions. And crafting a writing playlist certainly offers more sophisticated options than the generic chatter down at Costa (which is where I'm writing this).

Caroline Webb revealed in her book *How to Have a Good Day* that she regularly blasts out Donna Summer's 'I Feel Love' before she leads a workshop to get her into a positive, energetic mood. I asked her if she had a similar routine for getting into the writing groove.

> *'Of course, absolutely. I have a soundtrack for just about everything... [Writing needs] a particular type of playlist because your conscious brain, your deliberate system, can only do one thing at a time. You really need whatever playlist you are listening to to be something that you can process on automatic so that it doesn't get in the way of your thinking processes, your conscious thinking processes.*
>
> *'I was listening to Haydn's string quartets on a loop again and again and again. I knew them so well that I didn't really need to consciously engage with them but I associated listening to them with, "Oh, I'm writing now."'*

(She later got bored of Haydn and replaced him with instrumental deep house, which apparently is functionally quite similar. Who knew?)

Daniel Priestley creates a playlist before he starts writing each book – he too favours house – and finds it helps him focus and also get into the writing groove more efficiently:

'I like to create a playlist of just maybe 15 different songs, mostly instrumental, no words… and I'll put my headphones on, and I'll listen to that playlist on repeat while I'm writing… When I didn't have a playlist, it would take me a good 15, 20 minutes just to read back over what I was writing before, and to… get my head back in the zone. Whereas, when I had a playlist that was very distinctive for that book, it would actually trigger being in the zone a lot faster.'

Apart from the fact that music without lyrics works best in terms of not competing with your writing, this highlights two more key points of using music as part of your writing habit:

1. The mood and associations it creates for you.
2. The power of using a consistent signal to get you into the zone.

If you're not comfortable writing to music, you can enjoy both these benefits simply by listening to it for a few minutes *before* you write. This might even be more effective, in fact: there's research to indicate that even if you feel more productive when you're listening to music, that's likely to be an illusion based on the simple fact that you're having more fun.[26] (Though frankly if having more fun keeps you writing longer that's a reasonable strategy too.)

So creating your writing playlist is both an art and a science, and, ultimately, since so much depends on the associations and emotions a particular piece evokes in you, a very personal choice.

Over to you

- Take a moment to think about the state of mind in which you do your best writing: calm? energized? exhilarated? reflective? Then think of music that you associate with that state of mind. Classical and house work well as they don't have lyrics to distract your conscious mind, but there's no rule that says you can't have country *or* western if that's what works for you.
- Experiment: play the music in the background before you write and while you write, with headphones and without. Notice what happens, how it changes your state of mind, your productivity, your flow. Does it colour what you write, and if so how? And when you find what works, use it regularly until it becomes a cue to your subconscious that it's writing time.

---

[26] Perham, Nick and Vizard, Joanne, 'Can preference for background music mediate the irrelevant sound effect?' in *Applied Cognitive Psychology*, 2011, 25: 625–631. doi:10.1002/acp.1731

use a slide deck

Sitting staring at a blank Word document can be a killer. That's a lot of white space to fill. If you want to feel better about that, you have two options:

1. Turn up the font size to 50 OR
2. Make the white space smaller.

Allow me to introduce the PowerPoint slide.

If you're considering creating a course alongside your book, or even a talk, then it can sometimes help to start with the slide deck rather than the book itself. Don't worry about layouts or formatting or finding pretty pictures, we're just talking about a title with a handful of bullet points below for now.

If you already have a **working table of contents**, that will be your starting point for the structure. And then it's just a question of working out roughly how many key points there are per chapter/section (i.e. how many titles and therefore how many slides) and getting down the bullet points.

Bryony Thomas mapped out *Watertight Marketing* this way:

> 'The way that I tend to get through an outline structure is to go into PowerPoint or Keynote and put a headline and bullet point level as if I were going to present the whole end-to-end to somebody else. That for Watertight became the chapter and subheading structure. I would do that all the way through before you start writing a single word.'

209

It's a bit like using virtual post-it notes: you can move the slides around easily if you need to (and they take up much less wall space). One of my clients is using this technique very successfully at the moment, creating slides to outline a course which will be a revenue-generating activity (financial motivation, good) and which he's promised to deliver for a client (accountability, even better).

Guy Kawasaki has some great advice on preparing a presentation which he calls the 10/20/30 rule: no more than 10 slides, lasting no longer than 20 minutes, and no text below 30 point font size. He's talking about pitches, but the principle is sound. There's a limit to how many ideas we can take on board at a single sitting. It's not a bad rule of thumb to set yourself a limit of 10 slides, each with around five or six explanatory bullet points, as the maximum for any one chapter. And I wouldn't mind at all if it were a good deal lower than that.

What you do with your finished slide deck is up to you – you can prettify it and work it up into a full course, you can pick out one section or a few headlines and create a talk or presentation, or simply use it as a prompt sheet to help you write the book. In textbook publishing a slide deck covering the main points of each chapter is often provided as part of the companion website, as a tool to help lecturers convey the concepts to their class – if your book is intended for an educational or corporate market, that might be a valuable additional resource.

At the very least it can help with discoverability: SlideShare is a great platform for research so upload it there with a buy link to the finished book.

Over to you

How could you use a slide deck of your book's content:

- To help you outline the content?
- For training?
- As an additional resource for readers who need to present the concepts to others?
- As a talk you could give at networking events or conferences?

NINJA TIPS

Now you have all the basics in place, here are a few power tips from Extraordinary Business Book Club guests to give you an unfair advantage in the book-writing game.

You're welcome.

use a timer

If you find yourself regularly procrastinating over your writing, or if you struggle to get into flow, this is a great pro tip.

Several years ago I read a short book by Caroline Buchanan, *The 15 Minute Rule: How To Stop Procrastinating and Take Charge of Your Life*. Its premise is simple, but incredibly powerful: you can get through pretty much anything if you set a timer for 15 minutes and just start.

I bought a kitchen timer expressly for this purpose, and regularly use it to kickstart me into jobs I'd otherwise never get round to, such as decluttering the playroom.

I used a slightly different tool while writing this book. Francesco Cirillo devised the Pomodoro technique as a student in the 1980s, using a tomato-shaped timer to break down his work into 25-minute sessions with a 5-minute break after each. After four pomodoros, a 'set', you take a longer break of 30 minutes. (I'm not quite so disciplined, and also have to work around commitments to clients – if I even manage two good writing pomodoros in a day I'm happy.)

Grace Marshall uses this technique too (and she teaches productivity so she knows what she's talking about) – she discovered it was a great way to overcome the superficial mode we so often find ourselves stuck in and get into the deep work of writing:

'I set a timer and said, "All right, I'm going to write for 25 minutes before I go check anything else." Every time I was tempted to check [my phone], I would look and the first few times it was "Oh my God. It's

only been four minutes." Then another one, "Oh, it's only been another six minutes." Initially, it was every couple of minutes I wanted to check. Then gradually, I just fell into that flow and started deep diving. Then next thing I knew I looked up and went, "Oh, wow. It's been 20 minutes."'

Over to you

Experiment with a timer:

- What period of time works best for you – short enough to keep you focused but long enough to let you get into flow?

the series in disguise

One huge mistake many first-time authors make is to try to cram everything they know into their book. The book – and possibly you and almost certainly the reader – will likely collapse under the strain.

Productivity expert Grace Marshall put it well when I asked her for her one top tip for novice business book authors:

> 'See this as the first book you're going to write, not the last book you're ever going to write. Rather than, "I've got to write everything" or "I've got to write the best thing ever," see it as the first book, as a starting point.'

Takes the pressure off at a stroke, doesn't it? And it allows you to be so much more clear and focused in your message. In our ridiculously busy world, less really is more. Nobody will thank you for burying the nugget that will change their world deep inside a 100,000-word book.

If you're feeling that the book you're writing is getting too long, or too full, it may be better as a series. Then the question is simply which (short) book to write first.

Here are a few good reasons to consider a series rather than a single book:

1. You can write shorter, more focused books, more quickly. Which means each one is more likely to get done.
2. You can do each topic justice, rather than having to cut it down into a single chapter.

3. You can target your audience's needs much more precisely, which means it's more likely to be found and purchased by the people in the market for solutions to that problem at any one time.
4. You can cross-promote titles in the series: list the forthcoming titles in the front of the first and add to the series list each time you do a new one.
5. You'll almost certainly make more money from six books at £5.99 each than one book at £15.99.
6. On some platforms, such as Kobo, you can do an ebook box set which gives people another way to buy (Joanna Penn has a great blog on this, although it's primarily focused on fiction).[27]

So if your book is getting out of control, check it's really a book and not a series in disguise.

Over to you

If your book feels like it's bulging at the seams:

- Could it be turned into a series?
- What might that look like?

---

[27] ww.thecreativepenn.com/2016/07/06/create-box-set-bundle/

mind your metaphors

'The greatest thing by far is to have a command of metaphor. This alone cannot be imparted by another; it is the mark of genius, for to make good metaphors implies an eye for resemblance.' – Aristotle

We use metaphors all the time without even noticing them – her glass is always half full, he's building a successful business, she's on fire. They are the poetry bubbling underneath our prose; they act as bridges between prior knowledge and new concepts.

Metaphors are of great interest to authors because they can serve as a powerful shorthand – find the right metaphor for your book title, and you can create immediate engagement, curiosity, surprise, familiarity, and a whole host of subconscious positive associations. It can also give a natural shape to your book.

Chicken Soup for the Soul conveys nourishment, care, comfort, healing and love. That book could have been called *101 Inspirational Stories* – but it almost certainly wouldn't have sold as well.

Guerrilla Marketing immediately conveys action, excitement, doing things differently, making the most of whatever you have. The metaphor is extended throughout the book, with appendices including 'The 200 weapons of guerrilla marketing' and 'Information arsenal for guerrillas'.

The trick is to find the metaphor that's not immediately obvious – because obvious has no impact – but at the same time not forced. Lodge the question at the front of your consciousness then allow yourself to associate freely and be alive to possible connections and similarities as you go about your business – inspiration can come from the most unlikely sources.

Serendipity is a beautiful thing but it can't be relied upon, sadly. If the universe fails to present the right metaphor give it a helping hand – write down all the obvious, clichéd metaphors so they don't clutter your brain and push on for as long as possible, ideally with a friend or two (brainstorming alone is a dull, unsatisfactory business), finding more and weirder connections. If you start to dry up, go outside and force yourself to find parallels between your concept and a random set of found objects – leaves, cars, a children's playpark, whatever – to kickstart your brain, then come back and brainstorm some more.

(It may sound crazy, but I've used this 'forced metaphor' technique when facilitating problem-solving workshops with businesses and it's surprisingly powerful: 'Our team is like this acorn because... because... half of it is exposed and the rest is hidden in the cup, and... OMG, the folk at head office can't see how the customers react when we demo our product!')

Once you have a few good ideas, don't try to choose immediately: leave the flipcharts and the post-its up for a couple of days and see which ones grow on you, try extending likely metaphors to see how far you can push them before they break, test them on people in your target audience to make sure they're meaningful and appropriate.

Use metaphors with caution, though: when you find one that works it's possible to get so carried away with it that you forget it's not *really* the thing it's describing. Michael Neill is master of the metaphor, but as he puts it:

'Somebody had booked some time with me and they wanted to go through my metaphors, "Yes, but if it's a pot of tea, what does it mean when it gets too stewed?" And, "If it's like riding a bicycle, what if the front wheel is wonky? What does that relate to?" I spent a fair amount of time answering the questions until I realized that the best answer was, "It's a metaphor."… It's something like that, but not that; you can have 1,000 metaphors and there isn't a more right one. It's whatever gives somebody a glimpse of what you're pointing to.'

Over to you

To kickstart your ability to find metaphors, try that 'found object' exercise:

- Go outside or even just around the house.
- Identify five or so random objects.
- Force yourself to think of at least one way in which they are like your core idea.

build a boneyard

Patrick Vlaskovits, co-author of *Hustle* and *The Lean Entrepreneur*, introduced me to the concept of the 'boneyard'; in film-making it's where non-essential scenes end up. Not quite deleted, but not quite in the finished film either. In investing lingo a boneyard is where assets end up once they've been stripped of all the usable stuff. It's where stuff goes to die, basically, but you can pick the meat off it while it's there.

Patrick and his co-writer Jonas Koffler created a boneyard for bits of writing that one person didn't like but the other couldn't quite bear to lose.

> *'We had this long, long scrap file, literally 10,000 words. I went in there and I carved it up by section. I said, "OK, here's where we talked about this. Here's where we talked about this," and I made I think about 20 little 500-word pieces, like little seeds, and then we actually went back to the boneyard and looked, "Hey, does this fit somewhere?" Quite a few times we went, "Oh, hey. This actually fits right here." "This is a great segue for here," or, "This bolsters this idea here…" It was clear our subconscious had thought that… this thing had to be expressed, but the other puzzle pieces hadn't come out yet.'*

At first I thought this was a form of intellectual recycling, and no shame in that. But as I've thought more about it I think Patrick's absolutely right to describe those small sections as 'seeds': there's something organic about the way an idea grows, grafts onto others, changes and develops.

So kill your darlings if they're not working quite right, but don't dispose of them completely. Leave them in the boneyard and come back to them with new eyes and a clearer sense of the bigger picture when you're ready. They might have rotted, or they might have grown into something unexpectedly useful.

Over to you

- Create a 'boneyard' document and when something's not quite working right in your book, drop it in there.
- Once you've completed the first draft, dig into it and see what you can use.

email tips

How many emails do you send each day? Each one is a micro-opportunity to get people interested in and engaged with your book-writing journey.

One obvious idea is to add a note to your signature: 'author of the forthcoming book 'Title' – ask me for more information!' or something similar.

But here's a really ninja tip, which I owe to Elaine Halligan, who set aside Wednesdays for writing. Rather than putting up a generic out-of-office response that day, she took the opportunity to explain exactly what she was doing and share a little bit about the book: 'Today is my day for working on my book manuscript for *My Child Is Different*. I am only checking emails twice a day and staying out of my inbox as much as is humanly possible. If your email is urgent please do speak to my office manager [contact details] who will be able to help you. Thanks for your understanding.'

The result of course was that she became accountable at a stroke to a whole load of people who regularly asked how she was getting on with the book and who are impatiently waiting to buy it.

It's a lovely demonstration of the magic that can happen when you start talking openly about your book. One of the reasons I think it's worked so well is that it's unexpected. We're used to dull out-of-office messages; if we have any emotional reaction to them at all it's usually irritation but then to discover the person you're contacting is actually undertaking this fascinating project that you didn't know about invites you to find out more.

It's also responsive – they've emailed her so she's not being intrusive; she's just letting them know what she's up to. That's not a marketing blast, that's a conversation.

Over to you

If you need to set up an out-of-office message while you write:

- Consider using it to tell people what you're doing.
- Invite them to find out more.

BEYOND THE BOOK

Finishing the book might seem like all you can focus on right now, but it's vital to keep the bigger picture in mind. You don't need to wait until you type 'The End' to make it a key part of your business. Here are a few ideas on using the book that go beyond the book itself.

get your marketing collateral ready to go

If you're writing a book you need to be ready. Not just for the hard work and the self-doubt and the copy-editor's queries, but ready for That Moment. That Moment when the news story breaks that is an absolute gift to you, because suddenly everybody's talking about the subject in which you're an expert, and this is your chance to play the ball and take the public stage.

It can happen very quickly, and often very unexpectedly. Publicist Ben Cameron put it this way:

> *'Something can come up in the news one day and then it's old news the next day. You have to be ready, you have to have everything ready to go and then pitch it right away, as soon as something comes up in the news that you can comment on. You get in there and you comment on it and you talk to the media... If you don't do it quickly you'll miss your chance.'*

It doesn't matter if your book's not actually published yet; you can still seize the moment as 'author of the forthcoming [title]' if you have your marketing collateral in place.

The pitch is the cornerstone of most PR campaigns, and if you're responding to a current news story obviously you can't prepare this completely up front, but there's a lot you can do so you're ready to go at the drop of a headline.

Here's a basic marketing collateral kit for authors in the process of writing a book:

1. **A good picture of you** – not an Instagram snap or a portrait with your kids, a headshot by a professional photographer that immediately identifies you as someone who is credible, professional and worth listening to. You'll need hi-res and low-res versions for print and online respectively and it's worth getting a black-and-white version too.

2. **Boilerplate text** – basically just a bit of text that sits at the bottom of every pitch to give the journalist some background information, like a mini 'About' page on your website. Often a journalist will simply lift this and use it in the piece as it stands, so it's worth getting it right. You need to include a few details about you, the book, your business, and your contact details. Which means you need to create:

   a. **A biography** – a short professional biography that simply says who you are, what you do and why you matter in the context of this story. Write it in the third person and keep it factual. Highlight particular achievements or positions and any particularly relevant or impressive experience or educational credentials. Keep it as short as possible and include *only* relevant information. (See **'write your biography'**.)

   b. **Your book summary** – two sentences or so that communicate crisply and clearly what your book's about, who it's for and why it matters. You can use this in a phone call, an email, even in a chance conversation with a broadcaster or journalist. (Not to mention potential customers.) It's hard to distil the message of your masterpiece into just two sentences but you'll be amazed at your own clarity and the response of others when you do. (See **'write a summary'**.)

Once you have all that you're ready to sit and draft a brilliant pitch to a journalist at a moment's notice when That Moment – YOUR moment – arrives.

But you can do even more than that. Here's a couple of tips for real author PR pros:

1. **The cover** – OK, you might not have this in the early stages. But as soon as your book's taking shape and long before it's ready for publication you need to be working with your publisher or directly with a designer to get an image of the front cover design. You can tweak it later, or even change it completely if necessary, but nothing says 'This is a real book' more convincingly than a picture of how it's going to look. Don't just use it for press releases: stick it on your website, share it on social media, put a thumbnail in your email signature, get it out there and own it. (And you may find it a source of strength and inspiration as you battle through the final stages of the writing too.)

2. **Anticipate questions** – as Ben says, 'you know what they'll find if they google you; you can figure out what their entire knowledge of you is. From that you can pick out what their obvious questions are going to be and you can prepare for them.' Simple, but brilliant. You can even draft a few suggested questions for the interviewer to ask

you – as long as they're interesting and right for their specific audience or readership. Remember most journalists are pressed for time: the more easily they can simply lift your copy as it stands, the more likely they are to use it. If you're pitching to local radio or internet radio stations supplying sample questions usually makes for a much better interview too.

Getting these basics done up front will mean you're ready to take advantage of promotional opportunities even before the book is published. If you see a news story that you can speak to you can quickly shoot off an email pitch to a journalist with your take on the story. Make sure you include a juicy quote they can use along with the marketing collateral and offer yourself for interview.

While you're preparing for your moment of glory, it's worth taking a good hard look at your social media and your website; if they need brushing up do that *now* so that you can feel confident when you start promoting your book.

While it's great to be ready to go when your area of expertise hits the front pages, as Ben says:

'If you're blogging and working your social media consistently on your area of expertise, you may well be the person the journalist reaches out to even before you have chance to make the call.'

Over to you

- Get your marketing collateral in place: a good headshot (at high and low resolutions), an author biography crafted to showcase you as the author of this book, and your book summary.
- Check your social media profiles: do they reflect this biography and are the headshots consistent and up to date?
- Make it a habit to keep up to date with the news and look out for stories where you can contribute your expertise.

create online companion material

A book is a superb way of holding a reader's attention deeply and allowing them to engage with your ideas. When they finish, they will feel as though they know you and (if you've done a good job) like you and trust you. You, however, have absolutely no idea who they are.

Which is a shame because, assuming your ideal readers are also your ideal clients, you'd like the chance to build a relationship with them. One way of doing that is to provide points of contact to bring them from the offline world of the book to the online world of your wider platform.

And it works both ways: if you create online material associated with your book it doesn't just bring people from the book to your patch of the internet, it provides another way to help people discover the book via an idle online search.

One great way to do this is to **write a workbook** (see next tip), but that's not the only option.

You can start by simply creating printable versions of exercises or models from the book on your website, like Bernadette Jiwa's 'hunch log', a simple but beautiful template that allows you to track an idea from inspiration to implementation, featured in her book *Hunch*.

Or you can go beyond the material in the book and embrace the multimedia possibilities of the internet, as Melissa Hood, author of *Real Parenting for Real Kids*, did: The Parent Practice site includes not just a summary of each chapter and copies of the exercises but additional resources such as links, handouts and videos.

Daniel Priestley cleverly uses the irresistible appeal of the quiz, inviting readers to answer a series of questions online and see how they rank: he's used this successfully for both *Key Person of Influence* and *24 Assets*.

Guy Kawasaki created a whole suite of collateral around his book *Art of the Start 2.0* – a Slideshare presentation, spreadsheets and Word templates to download, videos of talks and so on. I asked him why:

> *'My concept here is to provide as many free touchpoints to the book, I want to reach as many people as possible as quickly as possible. Advertising can't move the needle. Only word of mouth can move the needle, so the task is to generate word of mouth.'*

Over to you

What online material can you create to complement your book?

Think in both directions:

- how can you use your online platform to point readers towards your book?
- how can you bring readers from your book to your online platform and into a two-way relationship?

write a workbook

Here's what I often hear from authors:

'I want this to be more than just a book you read. I want people to engage with it, to be able to reflect and scribble down thoughts and answer questions as they go: I know, I'll put space for them to write in the book!'

It's a good thought process, except for one big logical flaw: people don't like writing in books.

It's partly cultural: books have a certain status in our society (that's part of the reason you're writing one!), and it feels inappropriate to deface them. It's partly future-proofing: a book is an economic unit, we might want to sell it one day, or give it to a charity shop, or someone else might do so if we go under a bus tomorrow, in which case we'd rather it didn't include our honest self-reflection. And it's partly practical: traditionally bound books don't lie flat, which makes them hard to write in unless you're prepared to break the spine. (And if you are, we can never be friends.)

From the publisher's perspective – and yours if you're paying the production bills – there's another problem: it makes the book longer without including any more useful content and that makes every single copy more expensive to print.

And finally, the killer punch: if your reader's reading the ebook, rather than the print edition, they're going to hate you for all those blank lines they can't use.

So, if you're now convinced that leaving space for people to write in your book isn't such a great idea, consider a workbook instead.

A workbook has no cultural pretensions. It screams 'Write in me! Make me your own! I'm a workbook, so work, dammit!'

You don't have to pay to manufacture it (unless you want to), because the simplest and usually best route is a PDF that can be downloaded from your site, optimized for a standard A4 printer.

And perhaps best of all, it brings the reader from an offline experience of reading your book into your online orbit, which means you can start a conversation.

Glenda Shawley, author of *Founded After 40*, created a superb, beautifully designed workbook to accompany her book. It's effectively a blueprint for the reader's business, an invaluable free resource, and many readers have therefore been happy to provide their email address to get it. And from the moment that a reader cheerfully consents to give you their email address you have the potential for a relationship. She's also had a quantity printed and bound and sells them at events and from her website for people who don't want to take the hit on their own printer ink and paper stocks.

Here are her tips:

'Try to keep it quite simple and to be clear about where the link is between the workbook and the book. Are you going to put extra instructions in the workbook or are you simply going to use the book and expect people to have both open side by side?'

Glenda's book has a 'workbook' icon to show where there are exercises to complete, but she's designed them so that both can stand independently.

And even though the workbook's free, don't fret about people downloading and sharing that rather than buying the book. Brand the heck out of it, big up the book, provide other touchpoints (Glenda has a Facebook community, for example), and see it as marketing, not piracy.

Your workbook can simply replicate the questions/exercises in the book in a more user-friendly downloadable format, as Dorie Clark did for *Entrepreneurial You*, or it can include material that's not in the book – this is particularly useful if you're running out of space (but be aware that not everyone will bother downloading the workbook, so put your best stuff front and centre in the book).

With this book I've taken a slightly different approach: while I've put up some useful resources that you can download on www.thisbookmeansbusiness.com, I'm creating a separate companion book, a journal that business-book writers can use to structure their thinking and chart their progress.

Over to you

- Do you want your readers to engage actively with questions or exercises?
- If so, how could you put those into a workbook that complements the book?

from page to stage

There's lots of reasons to write a book, but one I hear again and again is 'to get speaking gigs'.

There's no doubt that a book makes you more interesting to anyone who needs to book a speaker: it's proof that you've developed your thinking and have something to say. The very fact that you're writing a book makes you more attractive as a speaker, so don't wait until it's published to pitch yourself.

But think about how your book and your talk fit together as you write to make the most of these opportunities at every stage.

You could start by crafting a talk from the key argument of your book as you work through the '**Get Clear**' stage: try it out in a small, friendly group first and see how it feels to articulate it. Does the argument flow? Do the stories you're telling engage the audience? Is the terminology you're using making sense to them?

Once you're clear on the overall structure and you're into the hard graft of writing, you can repeat the process for particular chapters or topics, zooming in to do a deep dive of a particular area, using the process of crafting and delivering the talk to untangle any knots in your thinking.

You might want to consider how each part or chapter of the book could translate into a talk in its own right, as this gives you a broader reach and allows you to speak more than once for a single organization.

This is a great way to help develop your thinking and the book. It will also give you practice at speaking and provide the opportunity for endorsements and video footage, both of which will come in handy later.

As the book nears completion and launch it's time for something more substantial: this is the moment to develop – if you haven't already – your signature talk.

A signature talk changes the game. Any number of people could give a talk on your topic of expertise: only you can give your signature talk (hence 'signature', it's as personal to you and identifies you as clearly as the scrawl on the back of your bank card).

The tone and structure of your signature talk will depend on your audience, but keep these principles in mind:

1. Ensure the talk is pitched at exactly the same audience as your book and your business. You want each to reinforce the other, not pull in different directions.

2. Make your **distinctive IP** the centrepiece of both book and talk: this is your key contribution to the conversation and you need to own it and showcase it at every opportunity.

3. Rehearse it until it's flawless: every gesture, joke, pause. Don't even *think* about using notes. A signature talk is a performance rather than a presentation. Having said that, customize around the edges: add a topical or local joke to your introduction, highlight why what you're saying is relevant to this particular audience, pick a story that's particularly appropriate to illustrate a point and so on. Guy Kawasaki says:

> *'You need to give a speech at least 20 times in order to get good at it. You can give it 19 times to your dog if you like, but it takes practice and repetition.'*[28]

4. Sell your ideas, not your stuff. For you the talk might be primarily a vehicle for book sales from the back of the room, or a way of getting people signed up to your next programme, but that's not where your audience is coming from. Try and sell to them and you'll lose them. Focus on delighting them and let the organizer do the selling for you (but make sure they're briefed to do so in advance).

5. Be you. It's your signature, after all. Let down your guard, tell personal stories, let them feel by the end as though they really know and like you, which makes them much more likely to trust you. When entrepreneur Michelle Mone delivers her signature talk she begins by confessing that every time she speaks she throws up with nerves just beforehand: she has the audience on her side from that point on.

Once you have nailed your signature talk you can stop offering to talk on any subject anyone's prepared to give you. Just like your book, your signature talk carves out a particular space for you at the forefront of the ongoing debate in your area, and that changes everything (but be aware the debate and your own thinking will almost certainly evolve, so don't get too comfortable there).

---

[28] *The Art of the Start 2.0* (https://guykawasaki.com/the-art-of-the-keynote/)

Over to you

- If you're at the early stages of planning your book, think how you can develop your thinking and get clear on your structure and flow by developing talks from your key ideas.
- If you're nearing completion, or even before, get your speaker page live, ideally including video footage of you delivering your talk and endorsements from those who've heard and love you.
- If you're near launch stage, nail your signature talk/keynote speech and begin pitching to organizations with the right focus and audience.

THE LAST WORD

Setting up a business and writing a book have a lot in common. They're both fiendishly hard work, and they're both potentially amongst the most rewarding things you'll ever do.

Something I hadn't fully appreciated when I began is that when you build your business around something you love and you begin to write about it, reaching out into the world to talk about it with other people who have something interesting to say about it, you open up conversations and connections that not only build your business and provide material for your book, but which bring with them a profound sense of joy. Quite simply, the process of writing this book has made my life richer and happier.

My hope for you is that this book will not only help you write your book, but make your business more successful and your life more joyful. It's tough to do it alone, though, so if you'd like more support, ideas and inspiration, why not join us in the Extraordinary Business Book Club, www.extraordinarybusinessbooks. com, or The Extraordinary Business Book Club group on Facebook?

And if you have a brilliant tip of your own for writing a business-building book drop me a line and I'll share it with others – you could even be the next guest on my podcast!

A NON-EXHAUSTIVE LIST OF CONTENT OUTPUTS

anecdotes/
personal stories
animation
app/game
audio books
blog post
cartoon
case study
challenge
checklist
curated content
(e.g. links)
dataset
debate
demos
diagram/model
ebook
email sequence
feedback
flier/brochure
guest post/article
'how to' guide

illustrated quote
industry awards
industry round-
ups
infographic
interview
list
live-streamed
video
manifesto
meme
news updates
newsletter
online courses/
elearning
online summit
photographs
podcast
polls
poster
predictions
press releases

Q&A
quiz
reports
review
slide deck
SMS
survey
talk/presentation
templates
testimonials/
endorsements
Twitter chat
Twitter story
user-generated
content
video/vlog
webinar
website
White Paper
worksheets
workshop

USEFUL TOOLS

A compilation of online tools recommended by me and other members of the Extraordinary Business Book Club.

Tools for organizing research
Evernote (https://evernote.com)
Google Docs (https://docs.google.com)
Google Keep (https://www.google.com/keep)
Pocket (https://getpocket.com)
Scrivener (www.literatureandlatte.com/scrivener)

Tools for productivity
Slack (especially for collaboration – https://slack.com)
Pomodoro timer (https://tomato-timer.com)
Prolifiko (https://prolifiko.com)
Trello (https://trello.com)

Tools for creating content
Call Recorder (for recording Skype calls on a Mac – www.ecamm.com/mac/callrecorder)
Canva (www.canva.com)
Dragon (for dictation – www.nuance.com/en-gb/dragon.html)
Skype (for interviews etc – www.skype.com)
Rev.com (for transcription – www.rev.com)
Stencil (https://getstencil.com)
Vellum (for formatting books - https://vellum.pub)

Tools for managing social media
Drip (https://www.drip.com/)
eClincher (https://app.eclincher.com)
Hootsuite (https://hootsuite.com)
MailChimp (https://mailchimp.com/)
Sprout Social (https://sproutsocial.com)

Channels for distributing content
iTunes (for podcasts – www.apple.com/uk/itunes/podcasts)
Pinterest (www.pinterest.co.uk)
SlideShare (www.slideshare.net)
SoundCloud (https://soundcloud.com)
Stitcher (for podcasts – www.stitcher.com)
WordPress (https://wordpress.com)

Crowdfunding platforms
Readership (http://readershipbooks.com)
Unbound (https://unbound.com)

Other useful resources
NaNonFiWriMo (writing community – http://writenonfictionnow.com/about-write-nonfiction-in-november)
VIA strengths survey (www.viacharacter.org/www/Character-Strengths-Survey)

ABOUT THE AUTHOR

Alison Jones is the founder of Practical Inspiration Publishing, helping businesses with something to say create superb books that are deeply integrated with their wider platform.

A veteran of the publishing industry, she worked for 25 years with leading companies such as Chambers, Oxford University Press and Macmillan. (She was Director of Innovation Strategy at Palgrave Macmillan until she left to set up a pioneering new partnership publishing model in 2014.)

She also provides executive coaching, consultancy and training services to publishers and regularly speaks and blogs on the publishing industry, is a member of the board of the Independent Publishers Guild, and host of The Extraordinary Business Book Club podcast for writers and readers of extraordinary business books.

ACKNOWLEDGEMENTS

Where else could I start what will be a *very* long list of thank yous but with the Extraordinary Business Book Club podcast guests – especially, but not only, those featured here – for their inspiration, for being so generous with their time and wisdom, and for being such fun to talk to. It's hard to single out individuals, but I am particularly grateful to Sherry Bevan, Bec Evans, Seth Godin, Melissa Hood, Bernadette Jiwa, Grace Marshall, Joanna Penn, Kelly Pietrangeli, Julia Pimsleur, Penny Pullan, David Taylor, Bryony Thomas and Robin Waite for their personal and professional support.

Thanks too to the members of the Extraordinary Business Book Club itself, and to my clients, authors, and graduates of my mentorship and bootcamp programmes, all of whom have given their support, encouragement and feedback so generously, particularly Lyn Bromley, Michael Brown, Elaine Halligan, Nicola Huelin, Alice Jennings, Joanna Pieters, Penny Pullan, Jane Unsworth, Fabienne Vailes, Donna Whitbrook and Louise Wiles. Their experience and advice can be found throughout this book.

The Extraordinary Business Book Club itself would never have happened without the unfailing cheerleading and no-nonsense advice of my wonderful sisterhood of support: Ginny Carter, Helen Dann, Julie Dennis, Suzanne Dibble, Mi Elfverson, Liz Gooster, Abbie Headon, Sue Revell (particularly you, Sue, I'll never forget that call!), Karen Skidmore and Sarah Buchanan Smith.

Natalie Price, Shell Cooper and Sarah Roughley helped me pull the book together with unfailing good sense and good humour, and it was expertly copy-edited by Catriona Robb and proofread by Jay Dixon. But, if writing a book is phase 1 and publishing it is phase 2, marketing is the equally important phase 3 and Laura Summers and her team, Helen McCusker and Judith Wise gave invaluable support here.

An enormous thank you to the This Book Means Business street team, for their support, their good humour and their all-round awesomeness: they're listed in full on the next page and every one of them is a superhero.

And finally, my deepest gratitude to the world's most precious people (to me, anyway): to Mum for making it all possible, to George, my unshakeable rock, and to Catherine and Finlay, my best work and my biggest distractions. Thanks for letting me get away from you all to get the damn thing written.

THIS BOOK MEANS BUSINESS – THE STREET TEAM

Suzy Astbury, Suzy Bashford, Cathy Betoin, Sherry Bevan, Ruth Blanco, Lyn Bromley, Miriam Brosseau, Michael Brown, Karen Brown, Regina Byrne, Liz Calder, Kathryn Carden, Claire Carr, Ginny Carter, Rosemary Clarke, Suzanne Collier, Robert Craig, Carole Davidson, Ken Dickson, Linda Duff, Jasmine Dumasia, Bec Evans, Jonathan Feldman, Rozynna Fielding, Celia Gaze, Michael Gilmore, Karen Green, Elaine Halligan, Jane Hardy, Tim Hartridge, Jenny Hassett, Cara Holland, Giselle Hudson, Debbie Jenkins, Alice Jennings, Jude Jennison, Thea Jolly, Angela Jones, Karen Knowler, Graham Le-Gall, Kellie Lucas, Lynne Philp, Dorothy Martin, Lisa Martin, Sarah Meurer, Kate Minchin, Patrick Mogge, Pilar Orti, Clare Painter, Joanna Pieters, Kelly Pietrangeli, Sara Price, Bogna Pro, Penny Pullan, Chris Radford, Tony Reid, Sue Revell, Narina Riskowitz, Sarah Rozenthuler, Louise Seabrook Scrase, Nicola Semple, Karen Shaw, Glenda Shawley, Karen Skidmore, Tracy Stonard, Michael Taylor, Heena Thaker, Niruja Thiyagan, May Ling Thomas, Johanna Vesterinen, Yasmin Vorajee, Chris Watson, Donna Whitbrook, Louise Wiles, Sue Williams, Judith Wise, Cathie Woodward, Charles Young. Thank you all!

BIBLIOGRAPHY

Allard, Ebonie *Misfit to Maven: The Story of Argh to Ahhh* (Practical Inspiration Publishing, 2015)

Allcott, Graham *How to be a Productivity Ninja: Worry Less, Achieve More and Love What You Do* (Icon Books, 2014)

Buchanan, Caroline *The 15 Minute Rule: How to Stop Procrastinating and Take Charge of Your Life* (Right Way, 2011)

Cameron, Julia *The Artist's Way: A Course in Discovering Your Creative Self* (Macmillan, 2016)

Canfield, Jack et al *Chicken Soup for the Soul 20th Anniversary Edition: All Your Favorite Original Stories Plus 20 Bonus Stories for the Next 20 Years* (Chicken Soup for the Soul Publishing, 2013)

Carnegie, Dale *How to Win Friends and Influence People* (Vermilion, 2006)

Clark, Dorie *Entrepreneurial You: Monetize Your Expertise, Create Multiple Income Streams and Thrive* (Harvard Business Review Press, 2017)

Cooper, Brant and Vlaskovits, Patrick *The Lean Entrepreneur: How Visionaries Create Products, Innovate with New Ventures, and Disrupt Markets* (John Wiley & Sons, 2nd Edition, 2016)

Donaldson, Julia *A Squash and a Squeeze* (Macmillan Children's Books, 2016)

Durham, Malcolm *Wealthbeing: A Guide to Creating Wealth and Enjoying Wellbeing* (Red Door Publishing, 2015)

Elbow, Peter *Writing with Power: Techniques for Mastering the Writing Process* (Oxford University Press, 1998)

Ferris, Tim *The 4-Hour Work Week: Escape the 9–5, Live Anywhere, and Join the New Rich* (Vermilion, 2011)

Gerber, Michael E. *The E-Myth Revisited: Why Most Small Businesses Don't Work and What to Do About It* (HarperBusiness; 3rd edition, 2001)

Gladwell, Malcolm *Blink: The Power of Thinking Without Thinking* (Penguin, 2006)

Gladwell, Malcolm *Outliers: The Story of Success* (Penguin, 2008)

Gray, Barbara *Ubernomics: How to Create Economic Abundance and Rise Above the Competition* (Brady Capital Research Inc., 2016)

Halligan, Elaine *My Child's Different* (Crown House Publishing, 2018)

Harford, Tim *Adapt: Why Success Always Starts with Failure* (Abacus, 2012)

Hood, Melissa *Real Parenting for Real Kids: Enabling Parents to Bring Out the Best in Their Kids* (Practical Inspiration Publishing, 2016)

Humberstone, Fiona *How to Style Your Brand: Everything You Need to Create a Distinctive Brand Identity* (Copper Beech Press, 2015)

Jiwa, Bernadette *Difference: The One-Page Method for Reimagining Your Business and Reinventing Your Marketing* (CreateSpace, 2014)

Jiwa, Bernadette *Marketing: A Love Story: How to Matter to Your Customers* (The Story of Telling Press, 2014)

Jiwa, Bernadette *Hunch: Turn Your Everyday Insights Into the Next Big Thing* (Portfolio Penguin, 2017)

Kawasaki, Guy *The Art of Social Media: Power Tips for Power Users* (Portfolio Penguin, 2014)

Kawasaki, Guy *The Art of the Start 2.0: The Time-Tested, Battle-Hardened Guide for Anyone Starting Anything* (Portfolio Penguin, 2015)

Keller, Gary *The One Thing: The Surprisingly Simple Truth Behind Extraordinary Results* (John Murray Learning, 2014)

Kellman Baxter, Robbie *The Membership Economy: Find Your Super Users, Master the Forever Transaction, and Build Recurring Revenue* (McGraw–Hill Education, 2015)

Kitchen, Tim *How to Get to the Top of Google: The Plain English Guide to SEO* (CreateSpace, 2013)

Knight, Warren *Think #Digital First: The Modern Day Entrepreneur's Workbook to Business Growth* (Filament Publishing; 2nd edition, 2017)

Krug, Steve *Don't Make Me Think: A Common-Sense Approach to Web Usability* (New Riders; 2nd edition, 2005)

Leighton, Allan *On Leadership* (Random House Business Books, 2008)

Levinson, Jay Conrad *Guerrilla Marketing: Easy and Inexpensive Strategies for Making Big Profits from Your Small Business* (Houghton Mifflin, 2007)

Levitt, Steven and Dubner, Stephen *Freakonomics: A Rogue Economist Explores the Hidden Side of Everything* (Penguin, 2006)

Levy, Mark *Accidental Genius: Using Writing to Generate Your Best Ideas, Insight and Content* (Berrett-Koehler Publishers, 2010)

Linden, Wes *79 Networking Tips for Fast-Track Success: Discover the Need-to-Know Advice to Catapult You to the Top* (Noah's House Publishing, 2013)

Lovell, Nicholas *10 Ways to Make Money in a Free World* (Portfolio Penguin, 2013)

Lovell, Nicholas *The Curve: Turning Followers into Superfans* (Portfolio Penguin, 2014)

Lovell, Nicholas *The F2P [Free to Play] Toolbox: Essential Techniques for Fun, Profitable Game Design* (Gamesbrief, 2014)

Marshall, Grace *How to Be Really Productive: Achieving Clarity and Getting Results in a World Where Work Never Ends* (Pearson Business, 2015)

McGinnis, Patrick J. *The 10% Entrepreneur: Live Your Dream Without Quitting Your Day Job* (Portfolio Penguin, 2017)

Newman, David *Do It! Marketing: 77 Instant Action Ideas to Boost Sales, Maximize Profits, and Crush Your Competition* (AMACOM, 2013)

Patel, Neil, Koffler, Jonas and Vlaskovits, Patrick *Hustle: The Power to Charge Your Life with Money, Meaning and Momentum* (Vermillion, 2016)

Peters, Steve *The Chimp Paradox: The Acclaimed Mind Management Programme to Help You Achieve Success, Confidence and Happiness* (Vermilion, 2012)

Pietrangeli, Kelly *Project Me for Busy Mothers: A Practical Guide to Finding a Happier Balance* (Orion Spring, 2018)

Priestly, Daniel *24 Assets: Create a Digital, Scalable, Value and Fun Business That Will Thrive in a Fast Changing World* (Rethink Press, 2017)

Priestly, Daniel *Key Person of Influence: The Five-Step Method to Become One of the Most Highly Valued and Highly Paid People in Your Industry* (Rethink Press, 2014)

Ries, Eric *The Lean Startup: How Today's Entrepreneurs Use Continuous Innovation to Create Radically Successful Businesses* (Crown Business, 2017)

Rubin, Gretchen *Better Than Before: What I Learned About Making and Breaking Habits – to Sleep More, Quit Sugar, Procrastinate Less, and Generally Build A Happier Life* (Two Roads, 2016)

Rubin, Gretchen *The Four Tendencies: The Indispensable Personality Profiles That Reveal How to Make Your Life Better (and Other People's Lives Better, Too)* (Two Roads, 2017)

Shawley, Glenda *Founded After Forty: How to Start a Business When You Haven't Got Time to Waste* (Practical Inspiration Publishing, 2017)

Thomas, Bryony *Watertight Marketing: Delivering Long-Term Sales Results* (Ecademy Press, 2013)

Vaynerchuk, Gary *Jab, Jab, Jab, Right Hook: How to Tell Your Story in a Noisy Social World* (HarperBusiness, 2013)

Waite, Robin *Online Business Startup: The Entrepreneur's Guide to Launching a Fast Lean and Profitable Online Venture* (Rethink Press, 2015)

Walker, Jeff *Launch: An Internet Millionaire's Secret Formula to Sell Almost Anything Online, Build a Business You Love and Live the Life of Your Dreams* (Simon & Schuster, 2014)

Webb, Caroline *How to Have a Good Day: The Essential Toolkit for a Productive Day at Work and Beyond* (Pan Macmillan, 2017)

Weiss, Alan *Breaking Though Writer's Block* (available as PDF download from https://www.alanweiss.com/store/books/breaking-through-writers-block/)

Wicks, Joe *Lean in 15 – The Shift Plan: 15 Minute Meals and Workouts to Keep You Lean and Healthy* (Bluebird, 2015)

Wilkinson, Amy *The Creator's Code: The Six Essential Skills of Extraordinary Entrepreneurs* (Simon & Schuster, 2016)

Zinsser, William *Writing to Learn: How to Write – and Think – Clearly About Any Subject at All* (Harper Paperbacks, 2013)

INDEX

Printed in Great Britain
by Amazon